Contents

The *Students Speak: Are We Listening?* DVD includes video of students telling their stories as well as other tools useful to colleges. Find it on the inside back cover.

Acknowledgments

This book is about community college students, as told by community college students — their lives, their goals, and their educational experiences.

That they have allowed their stories to be told through this book is a collective act of openness and generosity for which we are truly grateful. We thank the hundreds of thousands of community college students who have reported their experiences through the Community College Survey of Student Engagement (CCSSE) and the Survey of Entering Student Engagement (SENSE), both conducted annually by the Center for Community College Student Engagement.

Heartfelt appreciation also goes to the hundreds of students who have been so willing to be candid with us in focus groups and interviews about their expectations, fears, challenges, and hopes for their futures. We are in awe of the courage and determination with which community college students approach their college experience. In turn, we are strengthened in our own resolve to do all we can to help community college leaders take the steps needed to help more students prepare for college-level courses, learn the college ropes, persist in their studies, and finish what they start in the community college.

While this book is *about* students, it is *for* community college leaders whose mission and passion is to help students succeed. We greatly respect the college people who have been willing to look at their own data from the Center's surveys and from focus groups and to learn from both in order to improve their professional practice.

Special thanks to those who have opened their doors, allowing us to learn from their students, faculty, and staff through focus groups and interviews that have been part of the Center's *Initiative on Student Success.* In addition to bringing their students to the forefront, they were open to sharing their own experiences as they seek to strengthen student success.

The community college student voice is lifted up in this work through the support of MetLife Foundation and Houston Endowment Inc. We are indebted to those organizations for their belief in the critical work to ensure that more students progress successfully to and through community colleges. Their vision and counsel along the way have been invaluable.

Foreword

Community colleges continue to struggle to improve the success rates of their students. That this is the case is not for lack of effort. Colleges have invested considerable energy and fiscal resources in programs to increase retention and completion. At the same time, they have become increasingly aware of the growing body of research on effective educational practice and ways to enhance student success. Yet college completion rates have increased only slightly, if at all, over the past 20 years.

Kay McClenney and Arleen Arnsparger argue that this reality persists, in part, because colleges have not developed the habit of *listening* to their students — and therefore have not taken student voices seriously into consideration as they plan programs and services intended to serve those very people. But simply stating that colleges need to listen to their students is one thing. It is another to argue, as the authors do, that colleges have to learn how to listen systematically and well, giving authentic voice to students, particularly as they describe their own experiences.

In this book, the authors describe what good listening requires of college leaders. Specifically, they argue that college administrators, faculty, and staff have to learn how to listen systematically to a representative sample of students, not just to student government leaders. Colleges also must see beyond what students look like to appreciate how savvy students are about what works for them, and they must be willing to hear what faculty, staff, and administrators often may not want to hear. In other words, colleges have to learn not only to listen but also to listen well.

Once they do so, college leaders can learn much about what works. They can do so by better understanding students' goals and expectations, their sense of their own readiness for college, their concerns as they begin college, and how, over time, their experiences in college shape either their success or the lack of it. The authors then share with the reader what *they* have learned by listening.

Among the many things learned is the importance of early interactions with faculty and staff and how these earliest connections shape a student's sense of being welcomed and of belonging. Early interactions in the classroom play an especially important role in shaping students' sense of themselves as learners. Lest we forget, a preponderant majority of community college students start college academically underprepared, and many understandably question, at least privately, their ability to succeed in college.

But success is possible. The experiences of students tell us, if only we will listen, about *how* it is possible. The authors reveal how students learn to navigate the campus and deal with the often confusing, if not conflicting, information they receive about what they have to do to succeed. As importantly, the authors detail what students have to say about experiences that help them succeed. These experiences range from college orientation and student success courses to early and frequent feedback about their performance. Of central importance are learning strategies in the classroom that require them to work collaboratively with other students and enable them to benefit from academic support that is integrated into classroom experiences.

By listening and listening well, we can learn much from our students so that we can better understand what all of us must do to more effectively promote students' success. As McClenney and Arnsparger illustrate, we must work together to establish on our campuses a culture of connection, high expectations, student potential, and collaboration, with inquiry and evidence as guides for our actions.

Vincent Tinto, Distinguished University Professor
School of Education, Syracuse University

Lifting Up the Student Voice

Who best can describe the experiences of registering, enrolling, and beginning classes at a community college? Who best can explain the excitement, expectations, perceptions, and fears of new students? Who best can define a student's educational goals? Who best can tell us what it feels like to know that you've fallen behind in a class, yet you're afraid to ask for help because "they'll think I'm stupid?" Who best can inform our understanding of what really matters in promoting student success?

We believe students are the best sources of information about their own experiences. Since 2002, through the work of the Center for Community College Student Engagement, nearly 2 million community college students have spoken out about their college experiences — how they spend their time in college, the challenges they face that make it difficult to continue their education, and what happens inside and outside of class that helps them reach their goals (or not). Through the Community College Survey of Student Engagement *(CCSSE)*, the Survey of Entering Student Engagement *(SENSE)*, and the *Initiative on Student Success* focus groups and interviews with students throughout the country, students are speaking. *Are we listening?*

With almost half of community college students dropping out before the beginning of their second year, college leaders increasingly are focusing on the front door of their institutions. What needs to happen during students' first weeks in college, and even before their arrival, to increase their chances of finishing what they start? Students have important stories to tell about their experiences. Alongside each community college's own quantitative data about student engagement, learning, persistence, and completion, student voices can help point the way toward far better outcomes for many more community college students.

Inviting Students To Share Their Stories

Since 2007, *SENSE* has provided a snapshot of students' experiences from the time of their first contact with their college through the end of the third week of classes in their first academic term. The 2011 *SENSE* Cohort, a source of survey data for this book, includes 96,000 respondents who represent more than

Who Are Community College Students?

Community college students are recent high school graduates, workers returning to college to learn new skills, students transferring to and from baccalaureate institutions, and first-generation college students. They are honors students and students who are academically unprepared for college-level work. Most community college students attend college part-time, juggling class and study time with work and family responsibilities. Many are low-income students. Many are new Americans, learning English as their second (or third) language.

Characteristics of Community College Students

AGE: Community colleges serve a very age-diverse population, but the largest group comprises traditional college-age students.

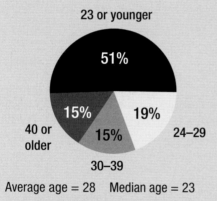

23 or younger

51%

15%

19%

40 or older

15%

24–29

30–39

Average age = 28   Median age = 23

SOURCE: STAKLIS & CHEN, 2010.[1]

GENDER: Women constitute a large and growing majority of community college students.

57% Women

43% Men

SOURCE: STAKLIS & CHEN, 2010.[2]

RACE/ETHNICITY: Forty-eight percent of all undergraduate students enrolled in U.S. public higher education institutions attend community colleges. Among those, the largest group is composed of white students, followed by Hispanic, Black, Asian/Pacific Islander, and students identifying themselves as Other or part of two or more racial/ethnic groups. The largest projected enrollment increase is among Hispanic students.

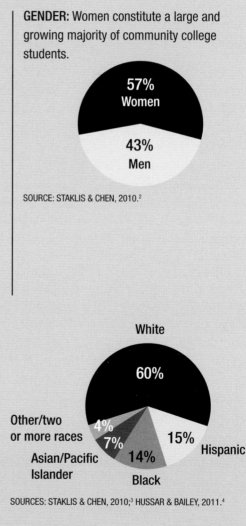

White

60%

Other/two or more races

4%

7%

Asian/Pacific Islander

15% Hispanic

14%

Black

SOURCES: STAKLIS & CHEN, 2010;[3] HUSSAR & BAILEY, 2011.[4]

EMPLOYMENT STATUS: More than 80% of students at two-year institutions work while attending school, with more working full-time than part-time. The percentage of students working to meet expenses continues to increase.[5]

ATTENDANCE STATUS: The majority (59%) of community college students are enrolled part-time.[6]

DEVELOPMENTAL EDUCATION/REMEDIATION: More than 60% of entering community college students report that their academic skills placement tests indicate they need developmental coursework in at least one area (reading, writing, and/or math).[7]

FIRST GENERATION: Forty-five percent of entering students report that neither of their parents attended college. (Source: 2011 *SENSE* Cohort data)

INCOME AND FINANCIAL AID: Nearly one-third of community college students have incomes below 150% of the federal poverty level. Approximately two-thirds of community college students receive some form of financial aid.[8]

1.8 million students from 217 community colleges in 39 states, plus the District of Columbia, Nova Scotia, and the Northern Marianas.

In the *Initiative on Student Success Starting Right* focus groups, we have inquired more deeply about students' earliest interactions with their colleges in order to better understand the perceptions, knowledge, skills, and experiences students bring to college with them, as well as their experiences as they progress (or do not) through their first year.[9]

To build this understanding, we have been inviting ourselves, since 2002, into community colleges across the country — colleges that are diverse in size, location, and student demographics. Most recently, we followed groups of students in six colleges through their first year, beginning at three of the colleges during registration. Through multiple visits and follow-up interviews, we listened and watched as students expressed their hopes and fears, charted their courses, changed direction, stumbled, struggled, made new connections, learned new skills, found support or failed to find it, and continued toward an uncertain future. And to learn more about the transition from high school to college, we also followed high school seniors as they anticipated their next steps in education and in life.

Everywhere we went we took our video camera. With students' permission, we captured both their voices and their faces as they answered our questions and told their stories. The DVD that accompanies this book presents video clips that bring students' stories to life. We invite readers to use these videos to prompt conversation within their own colleges and communities.

About *SENSE* and the *Initiative on Student Success*

The Center uses two approaches to better understand the experiences of entering college students. *SENSE* provides detailed quantitative data, and the *Initiative on Student Success* provides qualitative data. Findings presented in this book are drawn primarily from these two sources.

The *SENSE* survey is administered during the fourth and fifth weeks of the fall academic term in courses randomly selected from among those most likely to enroll entering students. The survey asks students about institutional practices and student behaviors during the early weeks of college that research indicates are associated with improved student success. (See www.enteringstudent.org.)

Through support from MetLife Foundation and Houston Endowment Inc., the *Initiative on Student Success* (www.ccsse.org/center/iss/index.cfm) conducted qualitative inquiries into the entering student experience. Through focus groups and interviews at colleges across the country, the *Initiative on Student Success* gathered the perspectives of both new and experienced students — as well as faculty, student services professionals, and presidents — to lift up authentic voices and build understanding that can promote student success.

Through the focus group series, the Center explored a number of themes and issues related to community college student success. Student participants are identified by host institutions based on the particular focus of interest and criteria specified by the Center. For example, if the focus is the first-time entering student experience, then the college will invite focus group participants who are representative of that subpopulation in terms of age, race/ethnicity, gender, enrollment status, college readiness (developmental students and college-ready students), program of study, academic performance, and so on.

Perhaps obviously, the findings from these focus groups may not be fully generalizable across community colleges; however, the themes that emerge over eight years of listening to students help to paint a compelling picture of their educational experiences.

Finally, it is important to note that the students have (and report) different experiences, often within single institutions and across both community colleges and high schools. Those differences reinforce the importance of colleges conducting their own focus groups — something the Center actively encourages. They point as well to issues of quality and consistency of each college's implementation of policies and practices intended to promote student success. And the differences serve as a clear reminder that students are individuals who need individualized plans and pathways toward achievement of their goals.

SENSE's rich survey data help colleges better understand *what* is happening at their college. Findings from focus groups and interviews can help them begin to figure out *why.*

The 2011 *SENSE* Cohort

2011 *SENSE* Cohort data include responses from 96,000 students who represent more than 1.8 million students from 217 community colleges in 39 states, plus the District of Columbia, Nova Scotia, and the Northern Marianas. Analysis indicates that *SENSE* respondents are generally reflective of the population sampled (students in courses most likely to enroll entering students) in terms of gender and race/ethnicity. In *SENSE* sampling procedures, students are sampled at the classroom level. As a result, full-time students, who by definition are enrolled in more classes than part-time students, are more likely to be sampled. To adjust for this sampling bias, *SENSE* results are weighted based on the most recent publicly available IPEDS data.

Starting Right Student Focus Groups and Interviews

Colleges:	14	Student Focus Groups:	101
States:	9	Number of Students:	7–20 per group, at least 25 per college
High Schools:	3 (Texas only)		
Campus Visits:	32		
		Interviews:	60

Other Voices

Students are remarkably savvy about what works for them and what does not. Further, what they tell us aligns with what emerging evidence from other sources confirms, as we will occasionally point out in the chapters that follow. The central feature of this book, however, is the voices of students, not the voices of experts, so citations of the literature are intentionally sparse. Ultimately, the message from students is that they clearly expect their colleges to know what works — and to do it.

Along with student surveys, focus groups, and interviews, the Center's work includes focus groups and interviews with faculty, student services professionals, and college presidents. Those discussions often reinforce the views of students, but sometimes they reveal contradictions, creating opportunities for campus conversations about diverging perceptions of the same experience. Occasionally throughout the book, we will offer examples of both matched and mismatched realities.

The other voices in this book are ours. While students take center stage in the following chapters, we, at times, insert questions directed to readers. The questions, and the point of view they reflect, emerge from our respective and shared experiences after decades of working with hundreds of community colleges. In addition, our observations are richly informed by work with an array of multiyear national, regional, and state initiatives focused on community college student success: Achieving the Dream, Completion by Design, the Developmental Education Initiative (DEI), the mathematics Pathways work at the Carnegie Foundation for the Advancement of Teaching, the California Leadership Alliance for Student Success (CLASS), Bridges to Opportunity, Student Success BY THE NUMBERS, Community Colleges CAN, Developing a Community College Student Roadmap, and others.

Our questions typically do not come with correct answers. Rather, they are intended to prompt campus discussions and to provoke questions about current educational practices.

The Rocky Trail from High School to College

Lydia, a student in a focus group, offered the observation that her educational journey had been like "a hike along a wilderness trail." Asked to elaborate, she said, "You know, it's like a winding path with lots of turn-offs where you can get lost, rocks that trip you, and thorns that hang you up, and fierce creatures along the way."

All too often, the transition from high school to community college, as students experience it, resembles that wilderness trail.

Few would argue with the observation that high schools and postsecondary institutions typically march to different drummers. From federal and state policies to funding formulae, from curricula to assessment, and from hiring practices to community expectations, the different sectors of the education system operate in separate environments that most often do not encourage collaboration. The experiences students describe as they leave high school and enter community colleges help us to understand how these divisions between education sectors affect students. Frequently, it is far from a pretty picture. In this book, we pay particular attention to the transition from high school to college, drawing hope from the determination of students and from the confidence that their experiences will inform improvements in the high school-to-college transition.

A Checklist Manifesto — and Beyond

Students in focus groups often speak about particular aspects of their college experience — educational programs or practices that have made a difference, often positive, sometimes devastating. Thus, as this book traces students' journeys through the first weeks or first year of college, it is organized around various phases of their experience, and it focuses on key educational practices.

One of the significant conclusions arising from the Center's work is that many community colleges are doing less than they know (or know more than they are doing) about what works in promoting student success. Thus, there is value in the notion of making explicit those practices that are supported by clear or emerging evidence as colleges contemplate serious redesign of students' educational experiences.

Addressing himself first to the health care community and then to much broader audiences, the physician and writer Atul Gawande wrote a powerful little book, *The Checklist Manifesto,* showing the results that can be achieved, in terms of human lives saved, when teams of professionals commit to clearly articulating evidence-based practice and then doing it — diligently, all the time, for every patient. It is not difficult to argue that similar discipline could be applied to good effect in community colleges — not for the health of hospital patients, but for the educational benefit of every student.

There is much to be learned from students' descriptions of their experiences with various practices — orientation, a student success course, a study group, or an advising process. What will not work, though, is for colleges to use this book — or a list of effective educational practices — as a checklist. It will not work to simply check off items ("done!") and move on. It will not work because success is unlikely to reside in any single practice. Success is more likely to be found in the *quality of implementation* and *integration* of whatever *combination* of practices the college *diligently* employs, *at scale.*

Throughout the country, community colleges are seeking ways to improve, designing and implementing interventions and evaluating their effectiveness. In this book, we include sample descriptions of how colleges — and in some cases, states — are taking steps to strengthen student success. The college examples are provided near the end of the book, so that as we read them, we still have student voices ringing in our ears.

In the end, college must not be about a collection of discrete practices. Rather, the challenge is to create clear and coherent pathways for students that more effectively facilitate student progress, learning, and attainment — pathways that engage, are built on and express high expectations, connect subject matter to students' lives and future work, and integrate academic supports into the learning experience. The strong and consistent student voice can help community college leaders meet this challenge. Let's listen.

CHAPTER 1

Anticipating College: Goals and Expectations

Each August, hundreds of thousands of aspiring college students crowd through the doors of community colleges, looking for their future. Many are students like Tina, a woman we met for the first time a week before classes began at a Texas community college. At 50 years of age, Tina had just been laid off from her job and was filled with uncertainty as she jostled her way through registration lines. Her daughter had encouraged her to sign up for classes at the local community college.

The same week, Frank walked through a similar front door at another community college, miles away in Virginia. A recent high school graduate, he had hoped for a university football scholarship. But his high school grades fell short, and his coach advised him to start at a community college, enroll in the basics, improve his grades, and increase his chances of playing football the next year.

During the past five years, several hundred students like Tina and Frank agreed to participate in the *Starting Right* initiative focus groups to talk about their college experiences.

Responding to questions on *SENSE,* community college students reflect on their earliest interactions with the college, from their first contact through the first three weeks of class. In focus groups, we ask students to step back in time and explore the perceptions and experiences they bring with them to the college that might influence their early encounters with college staff.

Hunched under heavy backpacks, invited students walk into the designated room to participate in their first focus group discussion. Their eyes scan the room and they smile nervously when they spot the video camera. They briefly acknowledge our greeting; they say nothing to one another. "Man, this room was hard to find," one student often observes. Others nod in agreement. We gesture toward chairs at a long table, and they silently take their seats. We introduce ourselves and explain our purpose. In these *Starting Right* focus groups, we tell them, we will be following their journey so community college leaders throughout the country can learn more about how to help new students get off to a good start in college.

In our initial meeting with students, we ask them to remember the first time they set foot on the campus where we are now meeting with them. Whether their first visit was on this particular day or weeks earlier, they easily remember their anticipatory thoughts and emotions:

"I'm 20. It took me two years to get to college because I was too scared to come."

"I was saying to myself, 'What did I get myself into?' I was totally lost. Because, when you sit on the job for 20-some years, you get stuck in that mold where you don't really need to learn anything else outside the box. Until you actually get laid off … ."

"I remember that I was so happy to come that I came five months before I had to. I didn't even finish high school [yet]."

The Faculty Perspective

Along with focus groups with new students, we also conducted focus groups with community college faculty. In these discussions, when faculty members describe their earliest interactions with students, the observations they share about new students are strikingly similar to what students report about themselves. As one faculty member says, "I see fear … walking … through each step. Some of them don't know where to go, particularly the first-time students. You can tell some of them are really scared when they first come in."

And so, amid anticipation, anxiety, and even fear, what do students have to say — about their goals, their expectations about college, and their motivation to succeed? Listening …

> "For me, when you go out into the workforce you see first-hand what you will have to live like without a degree, and what you live like with a degree. The jobs are better, the pay is better, the benefits are better; so that was my motivation behind going to college."
>
> — Community college student

I Have a Goal — But How Do I Get There?

Almost half the students who begin their postsecondary education in a community college leave the college before the start of their second year. Yet *SENSE* respondents indicate when they start college they expect to reach at least one specific goal. Nearly 80% say they intend to earn an associate degree. Almost three-quarters of students surveyed say they plan to transfer to a four-year college or university. More than half say they plan to earn a certificate. Students in focus groups talk about what led to those goals:

> "I [have] been working for the last four years right out of high school and it's getting harder and harder to find a decent job making decent money, so I thought that the best way to go about it was to go back to school."

> "College has always been like a must-do in my household. Like ever since I was younger, I wanted to be a doctor. The only way I knew how to do it was — you have to go to school, you have to take the classes and stuff."

> "My husband got laid off from his job, and I'm a stay-at-home mom, and I realized that job security, there is no such thing. So it would be better if both of us had a secure or somewhat secure career."

> "I wanted to have a job, a comfortable job. I didn't want some manual labor job that … paid minimum wage."

> "I just started talking to my parents … one night, and they was like 'Hey, you know, what do you plan on being?' and like I told them, I want to be an architect. And to be an architect, you need an education also; so that kind of set in reality checks. And I was like, well, if I want to be somebody and be successful, then college is the way to go, so that kind of sunk in, and I came here."

> "I'm a single mother, and I can't afford to depend on anybody else, so I knew that the only way for myself and my son to have a better future was to get a better education."

> "Really, nobody in my family ever graduated from college, so it's like I'm going to be the first … I plan on just having my own business. I don't plan to be working 'til I'm like 60 years old. I plan on retiring when I'm like 40, 45 at the latest. That's my goal."

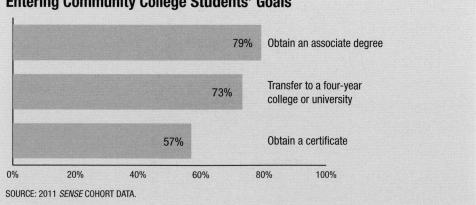

Entering Community College Students' Goals

- 79% Obtain an associate degree
- 73% Transfer to a four-year college or university
- 57% Obtain a certificate

0%   20%   40%   60%   80%   100%

SOURCE: 2011 *SENSE* COHORT DATA.

Students are quick to respond to questions about their goals on both surveys and in focus groups. However, as the conversation deepens, while students express certainty about their end goal — a degree, certificate, and/or transfer to a four-year institution — they often are far less certain about what they'll do with the credential they earn, and they typically have little understanding of what it will take to complete their studies at the community college.

Obviously, students offer a range of statements about their intended pathways. What is clear, though, is that many students — particularly those coming more recently from high school — need help from their college in clarifying not just where they are heading but also how they will get there:

> *"Honestly I have no idea. I have a bunch of different things that I want to do."*

> *"I don't know. I have no idea. Having my own house, hopefully. That's it."*

> *"Hopefully own my own restaurant or bakery 'cause that's what I want to do. I want to travel a little bit. I'll be doing some of that."*

> *"Going into law school."*

In focus group discussions conducted with students through their first community college year, a common theme is that students' initial lack of clarity about their educational pathway often results in missteps in courses taken and a sense of time lost while wandering through the curriculum. Listening over time to the same students, we learn that many initially selected a major without understanding what the course of study would require or even what the major would lead to in terms of jobs or further education after completing their work at the community college. Unsurprisingly, then, because they lack clear direction, students may either change their majors or return to the ranks of the undecided. They appear to be, and sometimes describe themselves as, "aimless" during their first year at the college:

> *"Still not too sure what exactly I want to major in but leaning toward the business side. I don't know, still got a little ways."*

> *"I decided that I didn't want to go with the major I was doing. I can't even remember what it was, honestly."*

> *"I just decided I wasn't interested in it."*

> *"It was a class I just had no interest in. And once I got started in that class, I dropped it immediately and was like, 'I'm not doing this.' Now I'm just trying to take cores and re-decide."*

When college leaders consider the processes they have put in place for entering students, there are important questions to consider: *Do those processes reflect an assumption that entering students have a clear picture about their educational goals?*

What changes need to be made in those processes in order to more effectively help students identify their career goals and create a clear and coherent pathway for achieving those goals? How quickly can colleges get students started on that pathway, so that their reasons for being in college are reinforced?

90% of entering community college students say they have the motivation to do what it takes to succeed in college.

SOURCE: 2011 *SENSE* COHORT DATA.

I'm Motivated!

Through *SENSE*, approximately 90% of new community college students say they have the motivation to do what it takes to succeed in college. In focus groups and interviews, they explain what drives them to succeed:

> *"College was never like an option, it was like you have to do it, 'cause I'm the youngest and everyone else in my family went to college — and my parents think that education comes first before anything. So college is a 'have-to.'"*

> *"College is just like a main focus since I was young, that's always been first. I just love to learn."*

> *"I've always wanted to go to college, but I had kids early so I had to … put them first. But I got into management, and … I was working too many hours, working 60 hours a week … . So I decided to just do it this year. I just couldn't hold myself back anymore."*

> *"Since I was little, pretty much, my parents would tell me to … get an education, go to college later on. I always wanted to go to college because my father … didn't get to finish high school. My mom just got her high school diploma, and I want to be the first, the first one in my family — for the girls, for my cousins — to be able to go to college. I want to keep going and get a degree."*

> *"I've always wanted to go to college. Nobody in my family has ever gone to college, so I'm the first — and I do it for my little brother, my little sister, and all my nieces and nephews."*

Before new students start class and in the early weeks of their first term, they consistently report that they are committed to do whatever it takes to achieve their goal. However, in subsequent focus group discussions during their first year, they often acknowledge that they didn't clearly understand in the beginning what it would take for them to succeed. As one student says, "I expected classes were going to be challenging but not as challenging as they came out to be."

The Faculty Perspective

In workshops and conference sessions throughout the country, college administrators, faculty, and staff wrestle with *SENSE* data, seeking to identify ways the data can help them help their students. Often, the first surprise involves coming to terms with the fact that the vast majority of community college students state that they have the goal of earning an associate degree or certificate. This reality prompts an important conversation about moving the college from a mission focused on access to a much more pointed focus on student success and college completion.

Also quite frequently, workshop participants react strongly to students' self-reported views of their own motivation. "They're delusional," one community college faculty member observes during a national conference session focused on the entering student. "Sure, they're motivated, but they have no clue," others often suggest. Many acknowledge that students *believe* they have the motivation to go to college and do what it takes to succeed, but they question whether students *know* what it takes to be successful:

> *"Students are so excited that they're here in college, they want to get their degree, and they kind of see themselves getting that degree in one semester."*

In related discussions, faculty members suggest that their older students frequently take on too much:

> *"I think our nontraditional students think that they're going to be able to take a full load, manage their families, their children, their husbands, their jobs, and they're gonna be able to juggle all of this, and it's gonna be great. At ... week two, it smacks them in the face, and they realize that it's not that easy, that there are a lot of different emotions going on within the family. They deal with the family issues, [such as] mom [used to be] there doing everything ... and [now] mom has to have study time and class time. There's a lot of stress ... . Expectations are high and then they tend to bottom out."*

Student voices readily convince a careful listener that these individuals typically arrive at college with high anticipation and the motivation to succeed. While they may still be terrified or uncertain about whether they really belong in college, they nonetheless are *there,* because they know that a college education will change their lives and their families' lives in positive and long-lasting ways. *How can faculty and staff harness students' early motivation?*

My Expectations about College

In focus groups, entering students talk about their own expectations, wonder aloud what's going to be expected of them in college, and express concern about whether they'll be up to the challenge:

> *"I'm expecting to get most of the work done in class. I do not want to take home a whole bunch of homework. I've got kids, I've got dinner to make, I've got a house to clean, I've got other things, you know."*

> *"Lots of notes, that's what I expect. Lots of notes."*

> *"I think it's gonna be a challenge."*

> *"I'm hoping for that challenge. I like to push myself mentally. I like to listen and learn new things, and I know that's what college is all about. They teach me stuff high school won't."*

Many first-generation college students have formed their expectations about college through a series of more or less dire warnings from high school teachers and counselors rather than through experiences that actually help them develop the requisite skills for success. So they may have vague understanding, which provokes both anticipation and anxiety, but they quickly learn that they do not have the skills to "do college" effectively.

Looking Ahead from High School

As they leave high school, few students say they have a clear picture of what to expect when they get to college. Their expectations, they tell us, come from teachers and counselors at their high school or from family members or friends who have attended college. Recent high school graduates talk about college in terms of the ways it will be different from or similar to their high school experiences. They also express concern about whether they have learned study habits and other behaviors that will serve them well in college:

> *"Honestly, to tell you the truth, I really don't know. I've never been to college, so I don't know what to tell you. I kind of expect it to be a little bit harder than high school ... and maybe a little bit more fun."*

> *"A lot more freedom, a whole lot more freedom, but it's a whole lot more responsibilities, too, 'cause you're on your own now. You don't have anybody to hold you by your hand and tell you exactly what to do step by step. So it's a lot of self-responsibility you gotta handle by yourself. But still I think fun and a lot of freedom."*

"I feel like … it's gonna be different, because instead of the teachers and other people nagging you to do things, you have to do it yourself. You're gonna have tutoring and everything, but you're gonna have to go for tutoring."

"I expect it to be a whole lot harder and not as much leeway. They just kind of baby you here. They say they don't, but they do anyway. They say, 'You're a senior, we're gonna stop babying you.' Then all of a sudden, it's just like, 'Okay, you didn't turn it in today. Do you have it tomorrow? No? Well, just turn it in before the six weeks is over.' I just don't think it's gonna be as easy at all."

"I think the big thing about college, I don't think academically it'll be too rigorous, but I think time management will be the only thing to make sure that you get everything done before you start doing fun things … . Fun things are definitely more appealing than sitting in the room and reading a book or doing something like that. I think time management will be one of the biggest challenges in college."

Often students describe what they *hope* college will be like:

"I hope they make it challenging so I won't want to slack off 'cause when it's not challenging I just — okay, whatever. Sometimes the teacher doesn't get into the class so you're like, they don't care about it, so why should I? I care about my grades. There's just some classes you know you can slack off and do good on 'cause you know it's easy. My GPA was a 93. During high school I didn't try. I catch things fast. So I would just do enough to have a good grade. If I really tried, I probably could've had a 100 but why bother? … I didn't have to try hard so I slacked off, but I knew I could. I still graduated top 10%."

My Instructors Want Me To Succeed

Several weeks into their first term, more than 87% of new students responding to *SENSE* say their college instructors want them to succeed. That said, it is important for educators to wonder aloud whether *wanting* their students to succeed translates — from the student viewpoint — into *expecting* students to succeed. In focus group discussions, students consider whether their instructors *expect* them to succeed and observe that it makes a big difference to them when instructors have high expectations for their academic performance:

"She tells you, 'You're doing good. You could do better, you know, you're a good student.' She makes you want to learn and do better in her class."

"It's a good feeling having someone knowing that you could do more, not just you're gonna be the average student. I'm not trying to say 'special,' but knowing you could do much, much more than what you're doing right now."

Recognizing the importance to students of high expectations from faculty, the question faculty members need to ask of themselves is: *Are we not only setting high expectations but also requiring that students engage in those practices that research and institutional data show make a difference in students' success?*

The Faculty Perspective

At a community college in Washington state, 10 members of the faculty sit around a table in the library. They consider the challenges of meeting the needs of the diverse students who come to their college. The conversation unfolds:

"We just know that students have potential, and what they need are skills to be able to be successful — and they have to learn those skills. And it's as simple as that. It's not that they can't do it; of course they can. They just need the skills and the tools to be able to do it."

"I think we whine and moan and complain like everyone else does. 'How am I supposed to do this? I've got a Running Start student and someone that's already got a master's degree and [is] coming back'... so I think we do what everybody else does ... and wonder how we're going to do it, but we all have the same mindset as far as expectations. It doesn't matter to me whether you're 17 or 67; these are the expectations, and I'll help you get there by whatever means we need to do it."

"But I think they know that."

"I think they do, too."

"I think that's why they're hanging in there."

"Our students have academic and socioeconomic deficits, but do we see them as coming as empty vessels? I don't think so. They come with their stories and all the kinds of strengths that they have as individuals and that their culture provides them. I don't feel that I know everything about philosophy, and I don't think that they know nothing about philosophy or speech or about culture and things like that. I think they come very rich. They don't often have the vocabulary to explain that or structures of organization to explain that or understand them in a more complex way. I think we spend a lot of time listening to their stories and valuing their stories."

But How Are Expectations Communicated to Students?

So students are motivated and believe that faculty members want them to succeed, and faculty members say they want students to succeed. A question then arises about how faculty and others at the college are communicating and reinforcing expectations regarding student behaviors that are associated with academic success.

On the *SENSE* survey, entering students report that they did the following at least once during the first three weeks of their first academic term:

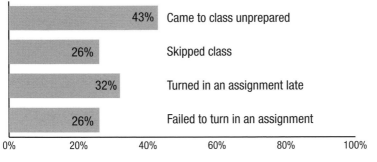

SOURCE: 2011 *SENSE* COHORT DATA.

As disconcerting as these data appear, there is even more troubling news when we disaggregate the data by age groups. On the *SENSE* survey, traditional-age students — those 24 years old or younger — report a much higher incidence of these behaviors during the first three weeks of class than older, nontraditional-age students. Consider the following data again, disaggregated by age groups:

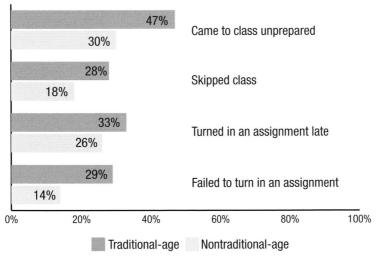

SOURCE: 2011 *SENSE* COHORT DATA.

Asked to describe their choices and behaviors during the early weeks of college, students confirm these survey findings. When asked follow-up questions, students often observe that they made these choices "because we can" — that is, because there are no apparent nor immediately obvious consequences. Recent high school graduates add that they were able to do those things in high school and have carried the habits into college. They comment further that in college no one is "nagging" you to do your work. "It's all on me," they report. When asked whether anyone talked with them about any of these behaviors during the first few weeks, most say, "no." However, occasionally a student in a focus group reports that he or she was shocked to receive a phone call from an instructor after he or she skipped class or failed to turn in an assignment. The student describes the conversation, saying the instructor expressed concern that the student would fall behind in the class, then emphasized the importance of attending class and keeping up with assignments. "What have you done since you got that call?" we typically ask. The answer? "I'm going to class and doing my work!"

Students in focus groups who indicate that they find a particular course challenging also report that they exhibit these early behaviors because they have fallen behind in their coursework so quickly. They say they do not know what steps to take to catch up. They simply stop attending class and/or stop doing the assigned work.

Taken together, these findings about students' aspirations and about student and faculty expectations set clear tasks for community college educators: identifying the ways that colleges can agree on and clearly communicate expectations both before and after students arrive; working with students to establish clear and coherent pathways to attainment of their goals; implementing academic policies that consistently reinforce high expectations; and very importantly, harnessing and sustaining the motivation that students bring with them to college.

Rachel's Story

Rachel has had it with negativity. At age 31, this wife and mother of two young daughters is determined to become a registered nurse and does not like being told it cannot be done. "Every person you talk to — whether it be a professor or a counselor — tells you, 'We have 80 to 150 applicants and only 24 can get in, and y'all are probably not going to make it,'" she says. Having completed almost two years of demanding prerequisites and carrying a 3.4 GPA, Rachel stands on the brink. If she is accepted into the highly selective nursing program, then it will mean at least another 18 months of asking her family to take a back seat to her studies. Rachel believes it is worth it. She started college when her husband was laid off from his job. "I [was] a stay-at-home mom, and I realized that job security, there is no such thing. So it would be better if both of us had a … somewhat secure career," Rachel says.

When her youngest started kindergarten, Rachel entered a community college, working toward a nursing degree. Though excited, she knew she had limits on study time: "I've got kids, I've got dinner to make, I've got a house to clean, I've got other things … ."

CHALLENGES: Rachel's first class, anatomy and physiology, began with a warning from the professor. "She said, 'Forty percent of you are going to drop out before the end of the semester,'" reports Rachel. "Maybe telling us is a good thing, because we study extra, extra hard, but it could be a bad thing. It makes you think, 'This is too hard for me … I just can't do it.'"

She says the warning was justified. The classes were hard, requiring more time than she had anticipated. "I need to constantly be studying to keep up with this. I don't want to just pass these classes, I want to ace these classes, but I'm having trouble balancing my time," she reported late in the semester. "My poor children. I studied all day Saturday, all day Sunday, and my 7-year-old would crawl in bed with me and poke me and say, 'Mommy, can I have a hug?' It breaks my heart," Rachel says. "I'm thinking, 'What's my priority here? Do I take a break and spend some time with my kids … miss out on that A and get a C instead?'"

FINDING WHAT WORKS: When Rachel's performance caught the eye of her microbiology professor, she was offered a half-time work-study job in the lab and worked closely with the professor. "She was able to help clarify a lot of things, to help guide me," Rachel says. "Being in a small community college, we do become friendly with our professors, and we're not afraid to ask questions. It is a very positive experience."

In addition to her own marathon study sessions, Rachel attended an optional weekly study group led by a former student who knew the material. "They advertise that it will actually give you a grade above what you would normally get, and I agree … . It really saved me big time," she says.

NEXT STEPS: Rachel says a number of her classmates have left school, changed majors, or are still struggling with nursing prerequisites. "I'm a survivor," she says, and she has become a role model for new students. "A lot of students ask me questions because I've been there and done that." With high grades and lab experience, Rachel is reasonably confident of acceptance into the nursing program.

Sarah's Story

Going to college was a given for Sarah; her mother graduated from a community college, and her father, a pastor, earned a master's degree. When Sarah enrolled in a community college after high school, she already had a definite plan. "I was just determined to be a nurse because it's such a good job, such good money," she says. Still, Sarah harbored some reservations about being around other college students, noting that she had been home-schooled since the 7th grade. However, she quickly found friends — and her future husband — at her community college.

GETTING STARTED: "I talked to a lady in the nursing department," Sarah says. "She didn't ask a lot of questions about me, really. She just got on the computer and mapped out my classes for the rest of my college. It was really nice to have somebody do that."

CHALLENGES: Working on a group project in her English class was new to Sarah, and she had some difficulty with other students she considered slackers. "If I'm going to be put in a group, I want to choose the people," she says. "It's not that I'm not mature enough to be able to handle being in a group with different people, but I just want to be with people who are going to be equally responsible in their classes."

Her first nursing requirement, anatomy and physiology, threw Sarah some curves. "I have never met anybody who had an easy time with that course," she says. Sarah failed her first assignment because it was late, even though she says the college website was down when she tried to submit it on time. "It irritated me badly," she says. "I told [the teacher] that I needed to know what I was gonna need to prepare for this class because I had a busy life. I have to work, I'm taking on a full load in college right now, and my mom's disabled, so I take care of my brothers a lot, also. He told me if I didn't study an hour or two every night, I wouldn't pass. Well, I just couldn't do that. I had three other classes that I needed to study for, too." Sarah made the difficult decision to drop the class.

Sarah began to suspect that nursing was not her calling. She talked to people in the field, found out more about the coursework, and eventually decided, "I'd rather do something that I'm more passionate about. Nursing wasn't it."

FINDING WHAT WORKS: Sarah found other courses that worked well for her, especially her first English class. "My teacher was amazing," she says. "Anytime we wrote an essay … she'd let us go back and revise it as many times as we wanted. She said if we were willing to do the work, she was willing to grade it and give us the grade we deserved — that the only way we were going to learn was through our mistakes. I really liked that."

NEXT STEPS: For now, Sarah is uncertain about her major. "I'm afraid to jump the gun on anything right now," she says. "I was so set on being a nurse. I've considered maybe doing teaching or something — I really love kids. I want to take a few more classes and see what I want to do." She has not sought out an advisor or visited the career center. "I feel like I'm pretty much okay right now. I don't feel like I need somebody to tell me what I'm gonna do … I'm trying to trust myself on it this time."

CHAPTER 2

Ready or Not

> "We get everything handed to us. They want us to succeed so much that they're like here, take it. I want you to do good. And that's not the way it necessarily should be. Because we keep on getting babied, when we graduate and go to college, we're on our own whether we like it or not."
>
> — High school senior

On a humid August day in a large Midwestern city, we meet Ismael, who is driving the taxi that takes us from the airport to a downtown hotel:

"Why are you in town?" he asks.

"To work with the community college here," we answer.

"That's a wonderful college!" he tells us.

He explains that he will be going to the campus later that day to register for his first classes. He describes the health care program he will be enrolling in and says the community college is known for it. He talks about immigrating to the United States several years before and his recent move into the city so he can attend this college and earn a degree.

His conversation is interrupted by his ringing cell phone:

"I won't answer that," he assures his passengers. *"It's probably one of my clients. I'm expecting a call this afternoon."*

"Your clients?" we ask. *"Do you have your own business?"*

"I'm a translator," Ismael responds. *"I work with companies that provide translation services for clients around the world."*

"What language do you speak?" we naively ask.

"I speak five languages," he answers. *"Two Indian dialects, English, French, and Italian."*

By the measures used in community colleges to determine whether students are prepared for college, is Ismael ready?

At the community college, Ismael will find himself sitting in class next to students who have recently graduated from high school, returning adults who are changing careers, students who are prepared for college-level work, and those who are not prepared.

In recent years, the median age of community college students has fallen. Nationally, the largest group of students enrolling in community colleges is now within the traditional college-age category — those coming directly from high school or within two or three years following high school graduation.

Considering the question, "Are you ready for college?" some recent high school graduates say that uncertainty about their level of readiness is a factor that has led them to the community college:

"I don't think I'm ready enough to be self-sufficient and leave home because my parents do a lot for me, and I don't want to leave that just yet. Also, maturing and realizing that, hey, I'm not going to have my family to help me, or, hey, I'm not going to be in high school where I can get away with everything. You have to become more mature in making that step and go to college if you want to be successful. And that's what I've been dealing with right now."

"The concept of going to a four-year university was like really exciting, but at the same time I didn't know what to expect going into college, so I figured I would just start at community college and work my way up."

"I feel somewhat ready, but I still think college is much more different than high school. So no matter what, you're not prepared because you've never been there in that environment. So somewhat prepared but maybe not … completely."

Are these recent high school graduates ready for college?

After working for 20 years in a series of jobs, Michael decides to go to college to pursue a new career:

"When I went to take the placement test, I passed everything just fine except the math part, and I want to be a math teacher, and I flunked the math part because I haven't used algebra in forever. [The developmental math class is] very easy for me, but I like it because I need a refresher course because I haven't been to school in so long."

Is Michael ready for college?

Whether a prospective community college student is an older adult returning to college or a recent high school graduate, what does it mean to be college-ready? Is readiness clearly determined by a placement test score? By the student's age? By an individual's understanding of what is required to be an effective college student? *And what is the role of community colleges in helping students prepare for success in college-level courses?* As we consider what it means to be well prepared for college and whether new students are college-ready, college leaders must ask a more important question: *Is our college ready for the students who come to us?*

85% of entering community college students say they are prepared academically to succeed in college.

SOURCE: 2011 *SENSE* COHORT DATA.

Am I Ready for College-Level Courses?

Responding to *SENSE*, 85% of new community college students *agree* or *strongly agree* that they are prepared academically to succeed in college. Yet based on the results of college placement tests, more than 60% of entering students need at least one course in developmental education to get prepared for success in college-level work.

How is it possible that students so commonly overestimate their academic readiness for college? The answer comes through in focus group discussions: Whether coming directly from high school or returning to college several years later, students believe they are academically prepared for college *because they graduated from high school*. Considering that fact, why would they not believe they are academically prepared?

Often students who graduated more recently from high school express surprise when college placement tests indicate they are not as prepared for college courses as they thought they were, particularly if they earned high grades or completed advanced coursework in English or math in high school. Their surprise is understandable given the findings from various studies looking at math scores on college placement tests. Studies of students who graduated in 2004 show that 17% of students who completed calculus in high school tested into developmental math.[1] As one student remarks when she receives her scores, "I've always been good in every subject I've ever taken, so it was like a shock to me that I was right on the borderline but at the same time a disappointment, 'cause I wasn't expecting to fail."

This disparity has led to a proliferation of national, statewide, and college-level initiatives aimed at correcting the obvious misalignment between expectations for high school graduation and criteria for success in freshman-level work. These initiatives address aligning standards and curricula between high school and college courses, rethinking college placement tests, emphasizing dual-credit courses, increasing the number of Early College High Schools (and other programs for accelerating student progress to and through college), and strengthening partnerships between community colleges and their feeder high schools.

Placement in developmental courses leads to mixed reactions from new community college students. Some immediately conclude that they are not in the right class and that it is "such a waste of my time and my money. I was pretty mad about that." Some students also say that being in a "remedial" class feels like "an insult":

> "I got a really low grade in reading, which now in my reading class, not to sound cocky, but I feel like I'm too smart to be in that class. I know what I'm doing. I know how to read. It just seems like I shouldn't be in that class. I should be in a normal class. I don't even want to go but I do — for the credit, of course."

> "I scored really low in math, and I just feel like it's a complete review of high school."

> "In the remedial classes, they place you down with the level that they think you need to learn from, but they need to place you with students who are gonna learn at the same pace as you. [I'm] in the lowest math class, but I catch on like that; I don't even need our book, I don't need to study, I don't even really need to show up except for attendance reasons. And then there [are] people in the class that sit there and for something that should take five minutes, 10 minutes to explain, you have to sit there for an hour and a half listening to him explain it again and again and again and them still not getting it."

> "He's a good teacher. He's very informative, but ... it makes me feel pretty dumb when I'm in that class because [there are] three of them, and I'm in the lowest one. And we're going over, to me, 3rd grade math, something that my little cousins can probably do. So I feel like it's kind of an insult to me, but I'm making good grades in there and everything, but it's just kind of like, wow."

> "If you're paying and if you're willing to learn, [then] it should be based on the speed that you're gonna learn at, too. It shouldn't just be based on what level you're in. Like in high school how you have the pre-AP® [Advanced Placement] and the AP, and I'm sure they have AP classes in college, too, but I think that they should put you with the same thinking level as other students."

Other new students say they are grateful for the opportunity to refresh their skills in a developmental class, even if they believe the coursework is not particularly challenging. Not surprisingly, this is especially true for students taking developmental math classes. Results from college placement tests identify developmental math as the need for the largest numbers of students:

> "In high school, I wasn't really good at math; I was really bad. So that's why I understood why I'm in a remedial class."

> "It's helping in getting everything back from high school that I had forgotten. I wasn't really doing any math."

"Yeah, it's exactly where I needed to be. I know a lot of it anyway, but it's mostly just touching bases again."

"I graduated in 2007, and I didn't take math my senior year of high school so I was glad for it 'cause I had forgotten some math."

"I'm like really bad in math. I used to get people to do my homework and all that stuff. So I'm actually getting it; so I'm like, 'Oh, that's cool.'"

"To me, the developmental math course is very helpful; it refreshes my memory on math, and so whenever I go into college math I won't be failing out of the class, 'cause I don't like math."

"I feel like it's a good step. I feel like I need it before I go and take college math."

Regardless of whether students are frustrated or satisfied with their course placement, among community college students who begin in developmental courses, 60% to 70% never go on to earn a postsecondary degree or credential or transfer to four-year institutions.[2] And many students end up failing and repeating the same developmental course time and time again. In addition, students express the simple frustration of spending semester after semester in pre-collegiate courses, which delays their progress toward achieving their educational goals:

"Without taking the — what did they call it? The pre? Yes, those [developmental] courses first, you can't even get to the college courses. You can forget about anything you need to get to the end of your classes for your major. I'll probably be in school here like three or four years before I even get to my nursing program."

Faced with the cost — in time, money, and lost income — of courses that do not earn college credit and lengthy sentences to developmental classes before they can move on to college-level courses, many students simply give up. When they first arrive at the community college, students believe they will remain in school until they move into a desired field of study. However, the data tell us that they do not.

Do I Have the Skills To Be Successful in College?

Even while expressing optimism about their *academic* readiness, entering students' focus group discussions reveal that students are not quite so confident about their ability to meet the different expectations they anticipate in college. Older students typically express concerns about how they are going to fit school into their already busy lives:

"Time management. Like I work, I usually work at night, and all of my classes are at night, so I gotta hopefully get those four days working during the day or something like that."

"I totally agree with that. I've got kids that I can drop off at school, then go to class, and then be able to come back and pick them up from school, and be able to be at home with them in the evening."

Recent high school graduates have a different set of concerns when they consider what it will take for them to succeed. In focus group discussions, they talk about whether they can demonstrate certain college-going behaviors that will help them succeed:

"I feel ready. I mean, pretty much my grades wouldn't explain how ready I am 'cause I slacked off a lot during the school years, my four years. But applying myself, I can pretty much make grades with the best of them. Once I get to college I'm gonna attempt more, try more, try harder in school. So yeah, I'm pretty much college-ready."

"In high school, even though we want to deny it, we get a lot of stuff handed to us. If we're not passing, they'll tell us to show up to tutorials; our teacher might give us a little curve. Once we get to college, supposedly as far as every teacher has told us, they're not gonna do that for us. And I've spent the last 12 grade years of my life getting everything handed to me. Not complaining about it, but that's just how it is. I know I can do it. I know we can do it. It's just I don't know how it's gonna start … and I'm a little worried about not having everything handed to us. You know, getting it for ourselves."

The Faculty Perspective

In college meetings, workshops, and focus group discussions, community college faculty share the same concerns that students express. They talk about the difficulty older students have balancing conflicting priorities. They also express pervasive concerns that students coming directly from high school have learned behaviors that do not work for them in college:

"I'll have students who come [to class] every day, but they're still behind, they're not turning in their homework, or they just think that if they just come and sit — and breathe — they're going to pass, or if they're nice, then they're going to pass, because they had that experience before they got here."

A series of mismatched perceptions reflects a clear finding from focus group work — that students, while highly motivated about going to college, often do not understand what is required of them to be successful. And faculty, meanwhile, appear to know this, but they are still figuring out what responsibilities community colleges have for helping students learn how to succeed and how best they can promote that learning.

Reality Strikes

"I'm in shock!"

In many instances, students' first college class experiences confirm the concerns they expressed before classes began about whether they have learned the skills and behaviors they need to be successful. Even so, as soon as they begin their first term, many students in focus groups express shock at the difficulty they are having in meeting expectations in their college classes.

Within the first few weeks of class, many students say they feel overwhelmed. They find that their courses move at a faster pace than anything they had previously experienced. Often, they do not know how to react. They believe they should be able to figure everything out themselves, but as the weeks go by, they fall further and further behind. As they describe their experiences throughout their first term, we learn that many are never able to get back on track. Their grades confirm the harsh reality. In sharp contrast to their initial affirmation of a commitment to succeed, many students now express disappointment, frustration, and uncertainty about their potential for success:

> *"A lot of my classes ... they have a set speed, and if you don't understand what they're saying at that set speed, then you can kiss it to a W."*

> *"My biology class is zoom, zoom. Soon as you learn it, you can't even retain it because you have to go to three more chapters in like a week. It's so fast."*

As students consider the challenges they now face in their classes, they say they are unsure how to overcome them.

Older students returning to college typically describe the difficulty of balancing conflicting priorities in their lives:

> *"Sixteen [credit] hours, and I'm married — I spread myself entirely too thin. I got in way over my head. And I was probably working like 15 to 20 [hours a week] ... and it was just entirely too much."*

> *"Time management is a big worry. I need to make sure I have an A on this upcoming test and my son is happy. And I have to have family functions, and I have to shop, and I have to maintain my home and clean. How can I get all this done? Basically everyday it's, 'Did I read enough to get me through the next class?'"*

Recent high school graduates raise different concerns about whether they have the skills they need to be successful. Once again, these discussions center on issues students commonly anticipated before they started college — issues that students say were even brought to their attention while they were still in high school. They say high school teachers and counselors "warned" them: "When you get to college, they're not going to put up with what we put up with here." But most acknowledge that they did not take the threat as seriously as they should have:

> *"All of my high school teachers said it was going to be hard. And they were pressuring me to get on the ball and do my homework and all that stuff. They're like, 'They won't accept it in college.'"*

> *"I mean, when you're a high school student, you don't take things seriously 'cause it's high school. Especially your senior year, you take a bunch of blow-off classes. All you really do is just show up."*

Despite warnings from high school teachers and counselors, new community college students express surprise at how different college is from high school. The expectations, terminology, and practices they find at the college are completely unfamiliar. Only a few weeks into their first term, younger students can readily delineate the ways that their daily high school experiences and choices failed to prepare them adequately for success in college. They quickly learn that behaviors that they describe as acceptable in high school are not welcome at the college.

Once they figure out that their old ways of operating in school will not serve them in the community college environment, they recognize that they do not have the skills they need to shift their approach. Even the most basic expectations — doing homework, going to class — sometimes appear to come as a jarring surprise:

> *"I'd been warned about all the challenges of college, and I believed that things were going to be a lot different, a lot harder, but I still didn't prepare, and I'm having trouble because of it, just keeping up with my work and stuff."*

> *"In high school, most of the time I just texted and didn't really pay attention, and you could get by. And college is kind of different because there's not somebody telling you, trying to stay on top of you, if you don't turn this stuff in, giving you double chances, stuff like that … . I missed one class and I missed two quizzes. Like in high school they give you second chances, third chances, fourth chances. And this [college] is all on you. So you basically just have to pay attention to everything because if you miss something, it's gonna hurt you."*

> *"In high school, I never did too much homework or anything like that; it was just what I'd do in school. And then, when you're in college, if you want to pass college,*

you need to study, you need to do all your work, and I wasn't used to that. I wasn't used to going home and making time for doing just schoolwork, and I had to learn how to do that."

Easing the Transition from High School to College

Recognizing that much more needs to be done to help students begin college prepared for college-level work, both high school and college leaders are expanding offerings of courses that help high school students and recent high school graduates develop the skills needed for college success.

Soon after beginning their community college classes, recent graduates easily distinguish between those high school experiences that prepared them for college and those that did not. Students' insights can be extremely helpful to educators as they design strategies to help students make a successful transition to college.

"My courses should challenge me."

Students who took more challenging courses in high school typically report in focus groups that their college classes are easier than anticipated. In particular, students single out courses identified as AP, gifted and talented (GT), honors, dual credit, and International Baccalaureate programs as types of learning they believe will serve them well as they go on to college.

Those students who experienced classes they refer to as "regular" high school courses along with more challenging courses report a marked difference in expectations, rigor, and acceptable behaviors. Students who completed the more advanced courses say they are accustomed to high expectations and to working hard:

> *"In AP… it seemed that the teachers put more enthusiasm into the work, that they actually cared. In regular [classes], it was just like do your work and see if you pass or not."*

> *"Non-AP courses, I don't want to sound arrogant or mean, but I really didn't have to put much effort into them. I just walked in and did what I was doing, and I had good grades, and I never actually got on borderline failing at all. But on my AP courses, I actually had to study. I actually had to work. We had homework, which is weird, because in my other classes they would assign homework, but I would be done with it before I got home, and with these courses I actually had to read. I actually had to spend time out of my day to actually study for them. And I actually did fail a test here and there. I also passed them, but it was a lot harder."*

More often than not, recent graduates who enrolled in more challenging high school courses acknowledge that someone pushed them into those classes:

"They made me get in them. My freshman year, I was probably in one AP ... not AP, pre-AP. And the teacher, she would push me and push me. She'd say, 'You know you're supposed to be in full pre-AP?' I was like, 'Miss, I'm a freshman. I don't even know really what that means. I'm just here 'cause they put me in here.' She asked me frequently, at least twice a week, and I'd be like, 'No, I'm all right. I'm good here. I think it's pretty easy.' By the next year, they told me a teacher had recommended me, and they asked me again if I wanted pre-AP, and I said, 'Not really. I think I like my schedule, and I think I like taking the easy route.' They pretty much forced me in it. I'm not complaining now. I'm glad they did. 'Cause if they wouldn't have put me [in the class], I wouldn't have learned as much here. Got anywhere as much experience. I think I would be kind of helpless, I guess. I wouldn't be prepared. So I'm glad they forced me in it."

Along with students who enrolled in more advanced high school courses, students who say they took a high school class specifically designed to prepare them for college, such as AVID (Advancement Via Individual Determination), recognize that they learned skills that will serve them in college and in their careers. They report having had constant conversations about college in those classes and say they completed portions of the college enrollment and financial aid application processes while still in high school. They describe filling out college applications and writing college application essays (often as assignments), as well as having visits from college representatives:

"They would tell me to go on and start now instead of waiting until you graduate and stuff. And I did. By the time I graduated, I was already ready to go."

"Actually, they wanted me to get in GT classes when I was younger. I said, 'No.' They asked me about AVID. I said, 'No.' I was trying to stay in my comfort zone. I enjoyed getting good grades with easy classes. Show my mom. She's happy, I'm happy. But they didn't even ask me [in] 7th grade. I looked at my schedule, and it said 'AVID.' This was before they even told me about it. I just saw it on my schedule and was like, 'What is this?' They were like, 'Oh, it's a college prep class. Enjoy.' Been in it ever since. I actually liked the class. The fact that they kept us so informed about stuff that I never knew about ... before I got in AVID. [They told us about] all kind[s] of scholarships that we can get in school. Main thing they taught me was how to be organized 'cause I was very disorganized. They taught me that."

Some students report that they were given the option of enrolling in more difficult high school courses but decided to take a less demanding route:

"I decided not to even go into the AP class where you have to take the test. All my classes from freshman to junior [year] were pre-AP. My senior year or junior year when I could take the AP, I didn't take AP classes. 'Cause I knew that I would

actually have to focus a lot of time on it. And it's like everyday homework, Monday through Friday, my friends had told me. I was like, 'I want to focus on sports. I got the grades. I just don't need to put more stress.' That was why."

"Our senior year is much easier than our first three years [in high school], I think. Unless you sign up to make it harder. Unless you, like, challenge yourself." — High school senior

"My teachers should expect a lot from me."

Recent high school graduates frequently talk about expectations that they believe were too low. They say they appreciate the teachers who had high expectations and went beyond "teaching to the test." Thinking about their high school's focus on testing, most students draw the clear conclusion that once they completed a state-mandated exam, often in their junior year, they were essentially done with high school. Worse, many also indicate that their teachers often confirmed that conclusion, either directly or indirectly.

Students talk about the impact of teachers who expected more — and the discouraging impact of those who expected little:

"I think they motivate students to not learn for just a grade, 'cause a lot of things are mostly results-oriented, just teach to the test and get that done with and go on to the next test … . And I think it works better when [they] motivate kids to learn just for the sake of learning instead … and when it would show up on a test I would know it because I enjoyed learning it. I learned it because I found it interesting, rather than I just gotta memorize these facts and then use them on the test. The grades would be just a side benefit that comes out of gaining the knowledge."

"It's a good feeling having someone knowing that you could do more than just be the average student. I'm not trying to say 'special,' but knowing you could do much more than what you're doing right now. I had high expectations from a lot of teachers. They knew I could do better."

"Some teachers just gave it to you too easily. They would give you the answers right away. They'd be on the whiteboard and working the problems with you. What are we learning from this? It just really bothered me. I just didn't feel challenged, and I feel that the higher expectations teachers have for their students, the better they are. I felt like sometimes teachers didn't care. Whenever they didn't challenge me, that's because they didn't care. That's just from my point of view. I like to be challenged, and that shows that a teacher cares about their students."

"Tell me I'm college material."

Not surprisingly, not all entering community college students say they were encouraged to attend college. In fact, students say the messages they received about what to do after high school depended, in large part, on the neighborhood they lived in, the classes they enrolled in, and the friends they chose. Some recent high school graduates say they did not hear much about college while in high school, often indicating that they saw more military recruiters than college recruiters at their school. Others say that college "was a big part of our conversation at school. They kept at it pretty much every day," and students were encouraged to attend sessions about college:

> "Like once a week with all the seniors … the counselors would come and give you advice, [tell you] what to do. And they'd have college nights; different colleges would come into our school and talk to us. Basically, my whole senior year was like a step up to college. So I guess that's why it's kind of so easy for me to transition from high school to college."

For others, the conversation about going to college was more discouraging, even from teachers and counselors at their high schools:

> "They said that pretty much I had a lack of brains. They said don't waste my money … just do what you can or [join the] military."

Some students say they wished they had received more encouragement to attend college. As one student several years out of high school explains:

> "That's why I'm starting so late, because nobody ever pushed me."

Some students point to discouraging words from their friends, bringing notes of poignancy to focus group discussions:

> "Jealousy. Well, I guess, you know how people think, 'Oh, they're gonna get big-headed with their education and think they're better than us.' So they kind of bring you down, but those are the obstacles that people warn you about. Your friends."

"I wish I had taken dual-credit classes."

Once new community college students learn how long it will take them to earn the college credits they need to move on to the next level in education or a career, many say they regret having turned down the opportunity to earn college credits while still in high school. At the time, they add, they did not quite understand the importance of those classes:

> "I have a little brother, and I'm trying to tell him, 'Your freshman year in high school they offer these dual-credit classes; take it. Because for one, it's less money coming out of your pocket. For two, it's a class you don't have to take in college. And for

three, it's better on you. It prepares you for what you're gonna have in college with the professors and the working, the studying, whatnot.'"

"If I could go back, I would do everything over again, I promise you that. Most likely I'd probably go back and take those dual-credit classes and take those college preps. But you want to get out of class early and go home. But the thing about it is, it's gonna set you up for later. But I didn't realize that. My focus was football, girls, and hanging out, partying … . 'Cause it was my senior year, I wanted to have fun."

"They didn't encourage you [to enroll in dual-credit classes], they just told you, 'You could do this,' and then they left the classroom and that was it. I didn't get the sense that if I took that class, later on in [college] I wasn't going to need to [take it] … I would have liked to do that."

Students Offer Advice to High Schools

Students understand clearly what they need to do to be successful. They also acknowledge that it is not easy to get them to do those things that will benefit them. Still, they are clear in their advice to high school teachers, counselors, and administrators:

"Advice for them is to stop babying us. We get everything handed to us. They want us to succeed so much that they're like here, take it. I want you to do good. And that's not the way it necessarily should be. Because we keep on getting babied, when we graduate and go to college, we're on our own whether we like it or not."

"Push [students] to get into programs that would be helpful for them to start thinking about college; that's helpful."

"I would say even create more programs for students that really don't too much know about college or aren't sure if they want to go to college. You create more programs, and it's gonna get more knowledge out there for kids to change their mind and to go to the next level."

Tending the Transition

The messages heard from high school students and from recent high school graduates are so clear and so consistent that they cannot be ignored. Low expectations of students abound. Negative messages about college are pandemic. Large numbers of high school graduates have not learned even the basics of the habits and skills that are — and should be — requisite to success as a college student. Yet when these students arrive at the community college, they typically are expected to know things they actually have no way of knowing.

As many community college and K–12 leaders now are demonstrating, the solutions do not lie in affixing blame. Instead they emerge from the kinds of genuine and painstakingly developed partnerships that are being established around the country, with leadership across the sectors. For leaders in both secondary and postsecondary sectors, the pressing questions include: *Are we prepared to come together as partners to solve the community's need to ensure that more students are college-ready? To what extent have we aligned standards for high school graduation with expectations for successful college-level work? How can we ensure that the community college's open-door mission does not send an unintended (and false) message — "no academic standards here" — to high school students? What can we learn from results in other communities?*

Meanwhile, community college administrators and faculty have their own set of inquiries to consider: *Are we serving the students we have or the ones we wish we had? Do we serve students well when we lower our expectations for them? Does this college prefer to affirm students' right to fail or to ensure their right to learn to succeed? What are the important elements of that learning, and how might the college make it part of every student's experience?*

Seth's Story

Seth is a hip-hop dancer with a passion for music. The budding young entrepreneur started his own DJ business while in high school and plans to pursue a business degree. He saw community college as an affordable place to take his required courses, but he had a rough start his freshman year. "I was just like, 'Eh, whatever.' I just worked and wouldn't really study or anything, and then I didn't do so good," he admits.

Over the past two years, Seth has reflected on the cost of taking the easy road in high school, has gradually learned what college requires, and says he has adopted some effective study habits.

GETTING STARTED: With a sister who works in the community college financial aid office, Seth had the guidance he needed to apply for and receive scholarships and a Pell Grant. He did not meet with a college advisor, preferring to rely on family members for advice.

CHALLENGES: College seemed manageable at first — "Easier than I thought," Seth says. He quickly caught on to the social part, making friends easily. But taking five classes and working two part-time jobs was increasingly demanding. "In high school, you just do what you have to do to get by. Here, I actually had to study and put more time in it," he says. The workload and prioritization both were problems for Seth. "Some of those tests, man, you study for them, but you get there and you're like, 'What? That wasn't on … .'"

By October of his freshman year, Seth was struggling, but he avoided asking for help from the tutoring center. "Nobody really wants to go in there and ask for help," he says. "When you go in there, you're like, 'Man, they're gonna make me feel stupid.'"

Seth earned C grades and failed two courses his first year, but he persisted. He took a developmental math class three times before he passed. "Looking back, I should have actually challenged myself a little bit more [in high school]. I took the lowest [level] math class that you can take your senior year."

FINDING WHAT WORKS: Influenced by parents who set the example — "They think education comes first, before anything," Seth says — he did not want to let himself off the hook. "I guess it's just my personality that I'm not one to just give up real easy. I wouldn't want to quit, because then I feel like I've just given up on everything I have going for me."

Seth finally found a way to study that worked for him. "As long as I'm in my room with my headphones on, I can study, I can block everything out," he says. "And that's really just what it was — finding my place to study, finding my own time to do things."

After two years, Seth is taking more challenging classes and has adopted some study skills that did not come naturally at first. He explains, "I just need to quit playing around, buckle down, and get down to business, really."

NEXT STEPS: Seth is trying to blend the business of school with the business of music. He is considering a university program in business/entrepreneur studies and working to bring up his GPA to qualify. He has not met with a counselor or advisor at either the community college or the university, continuing to rely instead on family members to help him figure out which courses will transfer.

Craig's Story

Craig is the first in his family to attend college, and he has lofty goals for his future. "I plan on just having my own business," he says. "I don't plan on working 'til I'm like 60 years old. I plan on retiring when I'm like 40, 45 at the latest. That's my goal."

In the aftermath of Hurricane Katrina, 19-year-old Craig relocated to Texas with his girlfriend and her family. He enrolled in a community college even though it meant paying out-of-state tuition.

Craig has some regrets that he is playing "catch up" at the community college he attends. He wishes he had taken advantage of dual-credit courses offered at his high school. If he had, "I probably would have even had my associate degree by now," he says.

For his first year and a half of college, Craig was required to take developmental courses. He chose not to enroll in the college's student success course until the spring semester of his second year.

Craig says most of his classes involve only lectures and note taking, and that he has never done group work in class or attended a study group.

GETTING STARTED: The first week after Craig enrolled at the college, he was recruited by Brothers for Brothers, an organization that supports men of color in college. A college advisor also steered Craig to the TRIO program, where he was assigned an advisor. "Either way I turned I got help, really. But … I feel like I really don't need help right now. If I need it, I'll ask for it."

CHALLENGES: After school started, Craig learned about financial aid when a sign on campus caught his attention. He was able to get financial aid and subsequently establish his residency, making college more affordable.

While he attends college, Craig works 30 to 35 hours per week and also handles the responsibilities of being father to a baby girl.

FINDING WHAT WORKS: Soft spoken and prone to keeping his problems to himself, Craig says he did ask for help in math and reports a positive experience with his teacher: "He told me I was doing everything right, but it was just careless mistakes that I made. He helped. Now, every time we're doing something in class, he asks me do I understand. That's real good," Craig says. "A good teacher is the type who doesn't want [anyone] to be left behind."

Craig says TRIO and Brothers for Brothers provide him with valuable exposure to future educational opportunities. Through these organizations, he visited Columbia University and New York University in New York City and took a weekend trip to Texas A&M University. He knows that when the time is right, he can talk to a TRIO advisor for more information.

NEXT STEPS: After taking the student success class, Craig now has a map showing the way toward graduation. Once he earns his associate degree, he plans to transfer to a university. He is not sure what type of job or career is in his future, but he is open to new opportunities. "What my [college success] instructor was saying was the truth: New jobs are starting every day," he says. "There might be a job that might work for me that hasn't been invented yet. You never know."

CHAPTER 3

Taking It Personally

"[This college] is really, really like a community. The old saying is it takes a village to raise a child. Everybody in the village is helping out, and it goes from deans, president, down to career services, people in student life — and I think that they do just a phenomenal job of making you feel like you want to be a part of this."

— Community college student

"Who Knew Your Name at the End of Your First Week?"

Early in their first term, new community college students respond to this question during focus group discussions. In some colleges, the students immediately answer: "Nobody, really"; "Just the people I knew in high school"; "Maybe one of my teachers, but that's all."

In other colleges, students enthusiastically begin to count off on their fingers as they make a list: "Well, all my teachers, for starters"; "A lot of people in my classes; I'm pretty outgoing"; "My advisor, I've been to see her at least 10 times already!"

"It's always important to put yourself in students' shoes so you're looking at it from their perspective," one faculty member observes during our visit. "It's 'What do they need?' not 'What can we give them?'"

In these colleges, students clearly got the message. From signage on the walls to consistently high

> "It's a community and they care, so that's why I'm still here."
> — Community college student

expectations and continuing support in the classroom, to a philosophy of treating everyone as co-travelers on the learning journey, students understood what was expected of them and what they could expect from others. As one student nearing graduation describes her experience, "This is a family I will always come back to for support and understanding. I know they'll always be here for me."

There is emerging consensus in the community college field that no matter what program or practice a college implements, it is likely to have a greater impact if the design incorporates certain principles. At the heart of these principles is the value of helping students make connections — connections to the college and its people, connections with other students, connections between students' coursework and their futures, and connections to all the services and opportunities the college offers to support their learning. Through a growing body of research and community colleges' own data assessing the impact of various initiatives, it becomes increasingly clear that one of the most significant contributors to improved student outcomes is the development of personal relationships.

In 2006, with funding from MetLife Foundation, the Center for Community College Student Engagement conducted focus groups with students, faculty, staff, and college presidents at community colleges that previously had been recognized for their exemplary efforts to improve student retention. Each college's *CCSSE* data indicated a high level of student engagement inside and outside the classroom on survey items that specifically addressed connections and relationships. A summary of the work, *MetLife Foundation Best-Practice Colleges: Building Relationships for Student Success,* highlighted the degree to which these colleges were student-centered and the intentionality with which they created a culture of connection.

Research and practice show that students need to begin making critical connections from their first point of contact with the community college. On *SENSE,* students respond to items about the first connections they make at the college — whether they felt welcome, whether staff members helped them with entering processes, whether they received information they needed to get started in college, whether anyone had been assigned as their "go-to" person. The results of those responses are reflected in the *SENSE* benchmark labeled Early Connections.

In focus groups and individual interviews, students inevitably talk about how much it means to them when someone — a person they can name — knows who they are and intentionally makes a connection with them. Reflecting on their first experiences at the college, entering students are quick to talk about all the connecting points that made a difference during their first few weeks of school. In this way, students reinforce what research and institutional practice are showing — that experiences fostering personal connections enhance their chances of success.

When asked to talk about their connections with people at the college, students often will name an instructor, other students, sometimes an advisor, and frequently someone who has an entirely different role at the college. In a discussion with new students at an Arkansas community college, students are asked to identify anyone who knew their name at the end of the first week of school. Their responses are typical:

"Shirl," one student answered.

"Yes, Shirl," all other students in the group agreed.

"Is Shirl an instructor?" we asked.

"No," the group answered.

"Is Shirl someone you met in one of the offices when you first registered for classes?" we asked.

"No," the group responded.

"So who is Shirl?" we asked.

"Shirl is a groundskeeper at the college," one of the students replied. All the others nodded in agreement. *"She knows everybody."*

The students went on to describe their conversations with Shirl — who, according to the students, always greets them as they walk across campus. She asks about their families, remembers if a child has been sick and asks if he or she is feeling better, takes notice of whether a student has not been around for a couple of days, and cautions him or her against skipping classes.

The best way to understand the value of personal connections for students is to follow them through their first experiences with the community college. The way students talk about those experiences reveals what is most important to them.

The Earliest Connections

For students who are planning to enroll in a community college immediately after graduating from high school, their first contact with the college often occurs before they leave high school. Students who have that early opportunity to connect often talk positively about meeting college representatives prior to their first visit to the campus:

> *"I remember last year, senior year, they would have two or three people, representatives from [the college], come to our school, and they would be in our counselor's office all day. And they would be there for any senior or anybody that wanted to go in there and ask questions about the college or help register to get in the college. They would be there for you."*

For many younger students, the first connection with the community college involves the students' parents, just as it often would if the student were considering attending a four-year institution:

> *"The first person that came to see [the college] was my mom — she doesn't speak English — and it was this guy at a table, he was handing out papers, he was*

Spanish, and he told my mom everything. My mom was like, 'I love this school,' because he helped her so much. So she told me, 'You're going there.' So when I came, he told me, 'Oh, this is the office, the registration is here,' so he was the one who really told us where I had to go first."

Welcome to College!

On *SENSE*, 72% of new students say they felt welcomed when they arrived at their community college for the first time. Only 3% *disagree* or *strongly disagree*. But a quarter of all new students (25%) provide a *neutral* response. That's essentially a large-scale student shrug on an issue that should be front and center in efforts to strengthen college retention.

"I'm just saying, first impressions are everything. You don't want to come into a school and it's boring and you're like, 'Ugh, I gotta sign some more paperwork, I gotta talk to this person.' You wanna go and tell your friends, 'Hey man, I went there and they did this.' Encourage more people to come."

What are the experiences that influence whether a student will feel welcome at the college and remain motivated to continue? Both through their survey responses and in focus groups, students report that there are many opportunities to connect with them that can make a difference.

Making Connections at the Front Door

Students' first connections upon arrival at the college are typically with college staff members in the offices where students go for admissions, placement testing, advising, completing the enrollment process, and applying for financial aid. At many colleges, new students report making numerous visits to these offices prior to and during the first weeks of college in order to complete all the necessary paperwork and processes. Even so, three weeks into the term, fewer than half of entering students responding to *SENSE* report that any college staff member other than an instructor has learned their name.

By contrast, students who do make a connection during those early visits clearly remember the people who helped them get started:

"When you find the right person to speak to, they'll make it more interesting, more appealing to you. It just depends on who you talk to."

"When I just came here I never knew what to do, where to go, because I just came on my own; my mother doesn't know anything about college or anything. But because of the big signs around the school … I was able to say, 'Admissions, okay, I think

I should go there.' And then when I went there, Miss Maureen, she was great, she helped me a lot."

"Two students that work for the school, they walked me around the school and they showed me everything. So I feel like I'm well-prepared to go here."

Students often cite college orientation sessions as potentially valuable opportunities for getting connected with the college. On *SENSE*, 11% of entering students report that they participated in an online orientation. Forty-five percent of entering students indicate that they participated in an orientation session on campus before classes began. Whether or not students participated in an orientation, they consistently talk about the importance of having personal contact as part of that experience:

"I actually liked it. It gave me the opportunity to already meet new people, 'cause that was also one of the things I was worried about was I didn't know anyone here. So I actually already made new friends."

"So basically get rid of online orientation … so they have more of a personal thing with a group orientation, and you also get to meet counselors and other students."

Forty-five percent of new students responding to the *SENSE* survey report that they never used academic advising services during the time from their first contact with the college through the first three weeks of classes. Seventy-seven percent of students report that they do not have a specific person assigned to them so they could see that individual if they need information or assistance. When students have not met with someone, they say they wish they had, and they express clearly the importance of finding someone they can talk to:

"I have one counselor in particular that I talk to, I know personally because she's personally helping me actually transfer because, like I said, I'm trying to go for film, so I've been looking at [a nearby university]. So then [I'm] trying to actually check off all the classes I need to take. So she sat down, and then she helped me out with emotional problems. Every time they'll give me a ticket for another counselor, I'll go back in line just so I'll get that one particular counselor 'cause she kind of knows me personally. So the thing about having a semi-personal counselor is you get that comfort of actually, okay, this is where we left off before, and you get that comfort of becoming semi another part of a family. You feel that connection … . I do have that particular person that I say is my counselor."

"It would be good if everyone had somebody they could talk to that is school-related and can help you in your personal and your educational life."

Thirty-four percent of *SENSE* survey respondents report that a college staff member helped them determine whether they qualified for financial assistance.

Here again, students point to the need for someone to work with them in person:

"Financial aid needs to have some personal assistance. At the financial aid booth, they kind of give you an overview of it, but they don't, for the most part, sit down with you on a one-on-one basis and go over everything you need for it."

Making Connections in the Classroom

For community college students, the classroom is the primary connecting point to everything the college offers, and their instructors are potentially the most important bridge to both support services and other relationships they will form at the college.

> "[Students need] community in your classroom. You help each other out, have a community."
> — Community college student

Almost all new college students participating in focus group discussions say they were nervous when they walked into their college classes for the first time. Recognizing that many community college students are older adults returning to school to further their education, younger students say they are worried that they will not know anyone in the class and wonder, "Will everyone be older than I am?" Older students, on the other hand, say they wonder, "Will I be the oldest person in the class?" All are wondering, "Will I fit in?" From the moment they show up for their first classes, they all are looking for ways to get comfortable with the college environment. As one young woman says, "I felt like it was sort of a terrible, wonderful mistake that I was allowed into college at all, and until I started getting to know some people, like instructors and other students, I just couldn't really feel like I belonged here."

On *SENSE*, fewer than half of entering students (46%) report that their instructors used activities to introduce students to one another. In focus groups, students typically say that their initial anxiety goes away and they begin to relax in those classes where instructors introduce specific activities to help them feel more comfortable and to get to know one another:

"When I walked in, there were new faces everywhere, but the instructor was really nice. She actually did this game, like an icebreaker … to ask our names and stuff, why we were here. And then, after we did that, she talked about what the class was going to be like and what would we expect from it."

"She would like pick something about the person and then connect it to remember their name. And then she'd be like, 'Oh yeah, okay, Alicia.'"

"The interacting with the students and teacher, it helps a lot here. I've noticed a lot of that in my classes — a lot of interaction, discussions, and just different things.

And then [other students] eventually come to you after class. They're like, 'Do you understand it?' You're like, 'Yeah,' and they become friends and study buddies, stuff like that."

Whether through planned activities in the classroom or through their own insights, many students quickly realize the importance of connecting with their peers. After their first three weeks of class, according to *SENSE* results, 82% of students report that at least one other student whom they did not previously know had learned their name. Eighty-six percent report that they learned the name of at least one other student in most of their classes.

Similarly, 86% of entering students report that at least one of their instructors learned their name by the end of the third week of class. In focus group discussions, students talk about the specific actions instructors take to make a connection with their students and how those actions make a difference:

"The first day was great because the teacher was well-balanced. You had young students and you had older students in the class, and the teacher was laid back. And I think because that first teacher made me feel so comfortable, it gave me a sense of, 'I'm on the right track.'"

"I've been out of school for almost 10 years, so I was kind of nervous coming in. I didn't know what to expect, so having teachers that are trying to get on a level with you is really nice, it helps you get involved more."

"I was so intimidated with my first class 'cause it was English 100, and I was like, 'I don't know anything.' But my teacher was really cool, and he walked us through it, and I would even go up to him after class every time I had problems or any type of question, and they just were there, they just were willing to help and everything."

"He's great, he's real hands-on with you, and he'll talk to you like you're equal, he won't talk down on you like you don't know anything. He's real straight up with you, and he's just great. You ask questions, he'll walk by you, see if you're all right. He's there for you no matter what, and he says it. He's like, 'If you need me for anything, not just for this class or anyone else's class, I'll try to help you out as much as I can.' I love that."

"She really seems like she cares about our opinions about things. And she always, whenever we come into class, I know it sounds really elementary, but we have this thing called 'weather check,' where she asks us how we're feeling and how our day's going. And it just shows that she really cares and wants to establish that good discussion forum with us."

"The instructor that I had this last quarter, she was fantastic. I mean, she gave us her [phone numbers], her email address, just anything that you wanted. And she said, 'Any time, you can call, leave a message, I'll get back to you.'"

"They are always open to people coming into their office[s], speaking to them, discussing anything about your goals, any type of problem you may be encountering with anything on the campus, or even if you have a personal problem. They're approachable, they're real people. And I just feel that that's one reason that I am so comfortable at the college."

By the end of the third week of class, 88% of new community college students report on *SENSE* that they know how to get in touch with their instructors outside of class. However, even though students know how to reach out to their instructors, many do not initiate contact, even when they need help in a class. Twenty-five percent of new students say they *never* asked an instructor for help regarding questions or problems related to their classes, 34% say they *never* discussed a grade or an assignment with an instructor, and 40% say they *never* tried to reach their instructors via email, text messaging, or any other electronic tool to communicate about coursework. Younger students — those 18–24 years old — are less likely to reach out to their instructors than older students.

Often community college faculty and staff assume that younger students will make far greater use of technology than older students in connecting with others at the college. However, when asked about their use of technology, younger students report being much more likely to use email, text, or other technology to contact other students, but they are somewhat less likely to use these electronic tools to contact instructors.

Students Offer Advice

"I think that each student some way, somehow, should be assigned to a mentor or something, because sometimes kids do get demotivated, and they need a little push, and they need the right encouragement."

"An open house, I'd say some time before school even starts. You'd get to meet your professors, and you get a sense of what they're expecting from you firsthand so you don't be surprised when you first get in class."

"I think the first two weeks of class they should have activities, different activities that get students to interact with other students, to get to know each other."

Making Connections Outside the Classroom

Whether attending the community college full-time or part-time, nearly 62% of entering students report that they are working for pay while attending school, and many also have family responsibilities. With such full schedules, these students often do not take the time to join organizations or participate in programs that would help them make connections outside of class.

Almost 90% of new students report on the *SENSE* survey that they are spending no time involved with student organizations within the first three weeks of their first term. However, in focus group discussions, new students quickly acknowledge that they need connections at the college beyond just attending class, and those who find their way to college-sponsored extracurricular activities describe the difference it makes for them:

> *"When I first came here I was very bored 'cause I wasn't associated with anybody. But then I started getting with the clubs, and I met my other family here."*

> *"I'm in Brother for Brother. Tomorrow we're having a black male summit, and we're having an induction ceremony. I do stuff. It's good. We do stuff outside of school. Like two weeks ago we went paintballing. We just do stuff like that. I'm good in a way."*

> *"I like the clubs because you get to participate in different activities and you get to experience different things and see new things. So you can apply that to your life and also make you a better person and make you more enjoyable."*

> *"They have the activity center so [you're] able to play, have fun, and, at the same time, learn."*

> *"I think there's a lot of opportunities to get the students involved. That's really good 'cause the more involved you are the better chances you have of staying."*

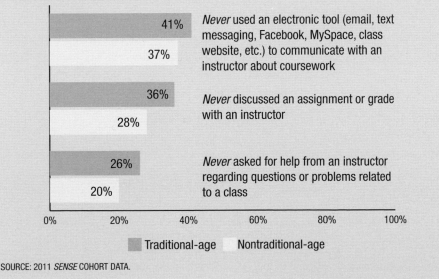

Entering Students Report that During the First Three Weeks of Class, They:

41% / 37% — *Never* used an electronic tool (email, text messaging, Facebook, MySpace, class website, etc.) to communicate with an instructor about coursework

36% / 28% — *Never* discussed an assignment or grade with an instructor

26% / 20% — *Never* asked for help from an instructor regarding questions or problems related to a class

Traditional-age   Nontraditional-age

SOURCE: 2011 *SENSE* COHORT DATA.

Even as students understand the need to become involved at the college and the importance of connecting with other students and staff, they typically do not reach out on their own. As college faculty and staff design the entering college experience, they must ask the question, *"How can we make these connections inescapable for students?"*

The Faculty Perspective

Community college faculty participating in focus groups often say they recognize how important it is to make connections with their students and to demonstrate that they care about each student and his or her success. They describe ways they try to connect with their students and create opportunities for students to connect with others at the college. They also speak to the need to forge those bonds during the first weeks of class:

"We do the 'chill and grill' where the students come and meet the advisors of the clubs and the other students that do the clubs. That should be week one … . I know it sounds maybe petty but three to four weeks into the semester they've already sorta got a routine. People are very ritualistic and once they've got a routine down they're good. 'I get it. I wake up at seven, I go to school, I go to the library, go home.' [By the] third week, it's too late for some students."

"Show them how much time you have for them. That's one thing. Whether it's five minutes after class — 'Hey, can I talk to you after class? Sure.' Whether it's the text message that you get on a Saturday afternoon. Whether it's online office hours or non-online office hours where you are still emailing students or having 'em drop by your office. I think that that's the most important thing. This is a big school, and we have a lot of students, so [we need to] show them that they still are people and that we have to give them personal attention."

"So I do encourage my students to communicate with each other. I say the first day of class, 'You're going to get to know these people because we're going to be spending a lot of time together. So don't try to act like you're shy, you don't want to talk.' I'm always talking to them or trying to make them talk."

"We've all had students that have come back to us, and I've had so many that transfer and that come back and say, 'Oh my God, the university is so different from the community college experience. Here you really seem to care about students, whereas there you're sort of a number.' But I think that's so important, demonstrating that you really do care about their success."

Faculty and staff often point to the challenges involved in helping students make the connections and develop the personal relationships they need to support their success:

"I'd like to see us be able to form more community among our students in the very beginning. I think we do try to do that. Some of the clubs and organizations we have on campus, the students get involved and get together. I had a student the other day tell me. I was just like, 'Why aren't you turning in your homework? You're here, but you're not really here.' And he said, 'I'm used to being on a basketball team, and I'm not on a basketball team now, and I'm just not motivated. Before I was motivated. I had teammates that would help motivate me, coaches that would help motivate me, faculty that would help motivate me.' So I think that would really be a key piece. It's hard. People just kind of come and go, and it would be really nice and I think very helpful for students to have that kind of sense of community. Not just among themselves but with the faculty and the staff. If we could do that more, it would be great."

Even without a basketball team, most community colleges offer a variety of opportunities for students to become involved, both inside and outside the classroom.

How can college faculty create connections in the classroom? How can faculty make it inescapable that students learn about opportunities available to them at the college and connect those opportunities to classroom learning?

The Reason We Are Here

On a faculty and staff development day at a Midwestern community college, a group of students takes part in a panel discussion to talk about their experiences at the college. The students come from different campuses of this large college, and only a couple of them know one another. They respond to questions from the moderator and from faculty and staff attending the session. They talk about situations at the college that had been challenging for them. They describe experiences inside and outside the classroom that have engaged them and helped them overcome challenges. An obvious and typical theme emerges in their responses.

The moderator asks the question we frequently raise in focus groups:

"Have you ever considered dropping out of this college?"

"I've thought about it a lot," one student answers, and the others nod in agreement.

"What's the single most important thing that keeps you coming back to this college?" the moderator asks.

Looking out at the couple of hundred faculty and staff in the room, one student speaks quietly into her microphone: *"You,"* she answers. *"All of you are the reason we are here."*

To students, it is clear what has the greatest impact on their success. Students who develop relationships with other students, instructors, and advisors, and who make connections to the college, have a greater likelihood of staying in college and achieving their goals. And students are looking to faculty and staff to help them make those connections. *How can everyone in community colleges intentionally create a culture of connection on their campuses?*

From students themselves, and through the growing body of evidence that shows the impact of college initiatives that help students make early connections at the college, we have come to understand that at every community college, everyone — regardless of their role at the college — has daily opportunities to help a student succeed. It is the power of making a personal connection with a student. It is the power of YOU.

> "The school has such a tremendous atmosphere. I think the president of the college sets the atmosphere and the teachers follow that atmosphere, and it makes the school, it just has a sense of pride. When I walked around, I had a sense of pride because the teachers, we started interacting, and they knew me and I knew them, and it was just great, it was great for me. It was a great journey for me, it was."
>
> — Community college graduate

Mark's Story

A talented athlete, Mark admits he skated through high school. He says that his teachers cut him slack academically; he even claims to have copied his way through pre-calculus, just to remain eligible to play baseball. "High school … was one big party," he says. "Over and over."

GETTING STARTED: College was a given for Mark, a family expectation. "I really had no choice," he says. "My parents and my sister were forcing me. I thought I'd just run right through it. Ace everything." Mark went to the nearby community college and met with an advisor, "… kind of an in-and-out thing, see what classes I was going to take."

CHALLENGES: Mark quickly realized that college was a different world — one he was not prepared for academically, and one in which his previous reputation as a star athlete gave him no special status. "It was easy to register," he says. "The problem was doing the *work* that I was supposed to do. I wish I would have learned in high school how to study and do my homework and all that stuff instead of waiting until the last minute."

Mark says his college teachers did not really get to know him. And he acknowledges that he did not make an effort to know them, either. Looking back on his first term, he admits, "To this day, I can't think of my teachers' names."

Mark says that, at the community college, he soon became a quiet, invisible student in the back of the room. "All of a sudden I was behind a couple of assignments. And then the next day, behind more assignments. And then after that, it was just overwhelming," he remembers. Unable to manage his schoolwork, Mark retreated to a familiar world where he knew how to be successful: sports. "I would just go play instead of do my work and stuff." Five weeks into his first semester, Mark dropped his classes and dropped out of sight. Nearly a year later, someone from the college called him to find out why.

FINDING WHAT WORKS: After leaving college, Mark got a full-time job as a mechanic and discovered that he loved working on automotive engines. He set his sights on attending a for-profit technical institute to gain job skills. "They said I'd have to get my basics first," he explains. Propelled by his vision of a future career, Mark found himself rethinking community college and re-enrolling, this time with a clear purpose: "to get into [the technical institute]."

With a course load that includes English, government, and college algebra, Mark is experiencing success on his own academic merits. "Like if I do a problem that I haven't done before and I actually do it on my own … I kind of enjoy it. It just feels good knowing I did something on my own that's right."

Friends are contributing to Mark's success as well. "I know more people," he reports. "I think that's why I'm doing a little bit better, because I have people in my classes that I know and that are actually making me come to class and do my work."

OBSERVATIONS: Mark believes his failed first attempt at college was a necessary step: "If I hadn't failed the first time, then I never would have actually known what to do this time. Now I know what to do, what not to do. Stay focused."

Daren's Story

His journey has been long, but when 34-year-old Daren, an Army veteran, graduates from the community college this year, he does so with a well-defined set of goals. His next step is working toward a bachelor's degree in biology, followed by medical school and a career as an emergency room physician. Daren's path was not always so clear; in fact, he recently changed his major from engineering to science. But life experiences have taught him that helping people is his calling. "For the first time, I'm actually excited about my life," he says.

STARTING AND STOPPING: Daren started college after graduating from high school, but he dropped out a few months later. "I wasn't ready for college," he says. "I made some bad decisions in high school and didn't apply myself because it was so easy. What kept me in high school was playing football and a weight lifting coach who taught me self discipline."

With few job opportunities in his small community and a long family history of military service, Daren joined the Army. He requested training as a combat medic, influenced by his volunteer work for a fire department rescue squad while in high school.

Daren served two tours of duty in Iraq, treating U.S. and Iraqi military personnel, as well as Iraqi civilians. While on leave, and shortly after getting married, he was diagnosed with post-traumatic stress disorder (PTSD). His marriage ended two years later.

RETURNING TO COLLEGE: After his military service, Daren was ready for a new direction. "I wanted to get away from all I went through in Iraq," he says. He enrolled in a technical school to become a NASCAR auto mechanic, but he soon decided he wanted to "be the boss" and registered at the nearby community college to pursue engineering.

Getting started was easy, according to Daren. "Everything went smoothly," he says. However, Daren still felt lost. "I didn't have a clue," he admits.

FINDING WHAT WORKS: Daren was placed in two developmental courses. "I thought only two remedial classes was pretty decent for someone out of high school for 15 years," he says. "I liked the remedial courses because it was an easier, slower transition to put me in the right spot, get some college courses under my belt, and build up my confidence."

He also enjoyed his English class, where, he says, "The teacher made sure he talked to everybody. He … gave us questions to think about, discuss, and debate." Daren also praises his algebra teacher for helping out "100%" if students did not understand.

He found support from teachers, advisors, and student groups. His program advisor heads the engineering program and has been supportive from the beginning, even helping Daren when he switched his major to biology. Another encouraging instructor showed an interest in his problems as a veteran and worked with him to establish a Veteran's Club at the college. Daren, who became student body president, discovered that help was available from many sources.

NEXT STEPS: Despite detours along the way, Daren now knows he wants to be a physician. His decision came unexpectedly when he served on a panel at a statewide educators' conference and was asked why he was pursuing engineering instead of medicine. "I began thinking more. For eight years [in the Army], I was helping other human beings and wanted to start helping people again."

CHAPTER 4

First Steps on the Pathway

"When you first register, you have the option to go see a counselor so you can see what kind of classes or how many credit hours you want. But that's optional, it's not required. I didn't do it because I already pretty much knew what I wanted to do."

— Community college student

"You're not required to go to the [advisor]. I've actually never met my advisor."

— Community college student

Students don't do optional! Often faculty and staff express frustration that their college offers many services and resources for students and the students simply do not take advantage of what is available to them. Perhaps surprisingly, students do not disagree. In fact, they are quick to confirm that they do not do what is "optional." They go on to explain that if the college tells them something is optional, then they figure that it must not be important. Since many students are busy people, juggling work, family responsibilities, and school, they do not choose to spend their time doing things that are not necessary or important.

Most prospective community college students do not know what resources are available to them when they arrive on campus to gain admittance and register for classes. And when they hear about options available to them, they must first figure out what the service is and then determine whether it will help them complete the enrollment process. "Do I need the financial aid office?" "Why should I see an advisor?" "Should I check out this website before I take the placement test?" "Do I have to go to orientation?" "What *is* orientation, anyway?"

Several weeks into their first college term, students already recognize that they did not do all they could and should have done to get a good start at the college. Asked to give advice to the college about how to strengthen the entering student process, students in focus groups consistently suggest that the college offer fewer choices for new students to make

"If you *know* what students need, and we don't, why don't you make us do it?"
— Advice to college leaders from a community college student

about which services and resources they will use. Instead, they suggest, "make it mandatory." When pressed about whether they really mean mandatory, students define the word for the focus group facilitator: "Yes, mandatory — that means it should be *required* for all students!"

Getting Started

Prospective students of all ages stream past the "Register Today" signs, crowd through the doors into the large, open space, and look around, hoping to find a familiar face or some indication of what they are supposed to do to get started at the college. Students talk about their first impressions:

> *"I said, 'Wow, this place is like an airport.' It's so big, people bringing bags and stuff, I'm like, 'Are they going somewhere?'"*

> *"All you see is just a whole bunch of people, it's like life just flashing before your face."*

> *"Kids walking around with backpacks and books and everyone just knowing where they have to go. Even teachers walking around like they're students with their little bags. It's cool."*

Though the room buzzes with people who seem to know where they are going, each new arrival struggles to make sense of the scene, trying to figure out where to go and what to do first. In many places, the physical space the prospective student has just entered reflects a college's earlier efforts to bring some order to the chaos. Large signs often mark the important areas that students coming to register are supposed to visit. An orderly line of computers along one wall beckons students. Sometimes a desk near the door carries a "Start Here" or "Information" sign, and an individual stands behind the desk, awaiting students' questions.

Trying to follow what others are doing, new arrivals take their place in lines, even if they have no idea what they are supposed to do when they reach the front of the queue.

The Student's Journey Begins

Students who are in the middle of the registration process are meeting with us for the first of what will be a series of focus group discussions throughout the year. How are they feeling as they get ready to start college?

> *"Nervous. It's not high school anymore, we're done with that, and it's time to grow up in the real world, and it's harder."*

"I'm really nervous, you know, being around a lot of young people. You sit in a class — you're almost 50 years old, and it's like, 'Oh God, what do I really know?'"

Admissions

Students' descriptions of the steps they've gone through in the college admissions and registration processes vary based on how they first connected with the college. Some students report that their experience has gone pretty smoothly because they completed most of what was required while they were still in high school:

> *"[The college] actually came to our school, and they broke us into groups based on what you wanted to do, and I wanted to get into teaching — so they put me up with a teaching counselor, and she actually picked out all the classes — and everything that I looked over, I wanted to do it. So then basically the only thing I really had to do was come and pay for my classes, and that was it. So I just came during August, paid for them, and I was all set to go."*

Many students take their first steps to enrollment by visiting the college's website. In some colleges, students say they easily found the information they needed and were able to complete part of the process before their first visit. More often than not, however, students talk about the difficulty of finding what they need on the college website:

> *"They do have information available for the college, but I found that trying to navigate their webpage is like trying to figure out a calculus problem when you have no clue what calculus is."*

When students are ready to enroll in the community college, many assume they can show up at the college during the designated registration days and complete the process in one visit. They quickly learn that their assumption was false. "How many of you finished everything you needed to do to get into the college in one visit?" we frequently ask. In most colleges, no one raises a hand. We keep repeating the question, adding to the number of visits. Two visits. Three visits. Slowly, hands are raised. During several recent college visits, we reach the number eight before all the hands are raised. These students had come to the campus eight times in order to do all that was needed to start college. *Are we listening?*

> *"The first time they made me wait like two hours, the second time they made me come back it was another two hours."*

> *"If you had to see an advisor, not only did you wait in a long line for two hours, but you waited another three to four hours just to see an advisor."*

"The advisor, they tell you what to do and then come back with the right stuff. Then again they'll tell you to come back with some more stuff and then to come back again. It's constant until when you finally get it you feel like you get that A, that passing A in class, that's how it feels."

For many students, each visit to the college means time off from work or hours spent in line trying to keep small children calm. Sometimes in meetings and workshops, faculty and staff suggest that students are not as motivated as they need to be to succeed in college. However, listening to comments from students who return to the campus time and time again serves as clear affirmation that they *want* to go to college, even if it means they must clear many institutional hurdles in order to get there.

In an effort to streamline the intake process, many colleges are redesigning their "front door." Some colleges choose a one-stop approach, and others create a welcome center. Many are reorganizing their registration areas, adding large, descriptive signs that point to offices and counters where students need to go; providing maps and checklists; and even, in some colleges, placing footstep decals on the floor so that students can follow the footsteps from one location to another. In colleges that have made strides in bringing some order to the traditionally chaotic registration process, students sometimes notice the guideposts, but many still report that the process was challenging:

"This college is like an airport in a foreign country. There are a whole lot of people rushing around, looking as though they know where they're going. But even when I see signs telling me where to go, they're written in a language I don't understand."

"I actually had no idea what to do, to be honest. It was very confusing, I got lost very easily. Even though I had a map — the buildings didn't have room numbers, and there were like three floors to each building."

Students' comments point to improvements in the process that would help them:

"It would be a good idea if we had maybe a line on the ground leading into the admission office so that you know where it is. But I would like something more about where it is that we're supposed to go when we first walk through the doors, because you just kind of stand around and try to read the letters on the wall and decide where you're supposed to go."

"For people like me who have never been here, I was totally lost … . 'Cause there wasn't anybody there asking can they help you, which way you need to go, what you need to do first. It was just you come in and try to find your way through. You've got people who have never been here, and you need some kind of system. [Otherwise] you spend all your time here wasting time in this line when you need to be over here in this line for another hour or two."

> *"There's nothing out there indicating for a person that's new … what I'm supposed to do besides register for class. There's nothing out there indicating where we're gonna have orientation tonight … you can meet the teachers this night. [There's] nothing out there besides just get your classes and try to find them."*

What becomes obvious in student focus group discussions is that no matter how well organized and simple to navigate the college makes the entering process, students are still lost and confused. Regardless of how clear the maps, the footsteps, and the signage might be, students do not have a frame of reference, the prior experience, or the language to help them understand what it all means. What is the purpose of what they're asked to do during the registration process? How will participating in placement testing, orientation, or other experiences impact their first weeks and first year in college? What should they be discussing with an advisor? What does matriculation mean? Just how long should this process take, anyway? No one explains the big picture and how each piece of the puzzle fits into it. Many students say they are not even sure what questions to ask to figure out what they should be doing or, even more importantly, why they should be doing it. They add that they do not want to look "stupid" by asking about things that college staff seem to think they should already know. *Given that lack of understanding and experience on the part of students, is it a surprise that they do not navigate the process easily or take advantage of the resources available to help them?*

In discussions with those who have just completed the registration process at their college, students reporting the best experience typically have something in common: They brought someone with them when they came to register. Sometimes the companion is a family member, sometimes a friend, but it is always a person who has previously been through the experience of registering for college. Students report that having a personal guide through the process made all the difference. *What about those students who do not have anyone to bring with them?* Frequently, these students are the first in their family or the first in their circle of friends to go to college. *Where will they find the help they need?*

Infrequently, students report that they found the guidance they needed to navigate the registration process from people who work at the college:

> *"It was a breeze. Everybody showed me step-by-step everything that I had to do. They basically took me by my hand and said, 'This is what you need to do, this is what we need you to do,' and it was very helpful. They made the appointments to see you when you need to be seen. As long as you're there, they're there to help you."*

Students express relief when they find someone at the college who can help them. Sometimes that person is a staff member; sometimes it is a more experienced student. Those who report having a good experience during the registration process talk about the elements that made it work for them:

"We liked how everything was organized and all together. The application had a list of everything you had to have. [There] was a hometown feeling — everybody knew who you [were] or if they didn't, they'd act like you were some lost relative. If you have a question, no matter what it is, there's always someone to answer it."

"Easy registration — if you didn't have it right there, in the end, they still let you register; as long as you brought it in before the first day of school, everything was fine. The layout of the campus — they made sure that you got a map of the school so that you could figure out where your classes were ahead of time, so when you came here the first time you weren't just like, 'Where do I need to go?'"

The Faculty Perspective

Students repeatedly say they would like to meet teachers before classes begin so they can learn what will be expected of them in college. However, in most colleges, faculty members report that they do not have a role in the entering student processes and have little interaction with students before the first day of class. Many say they are unfamiliar with the steps students have taken to get admitted to college and register for classes. As one faculty member acknowledges, "Being here for 10 years, I probably know less than I should about that process." Asked if they know what the registration experience is like for new students, faculty typically report not direct knowledge, but what they hear from their students:

"Whether you're a re-entry student or fresh out of high school, I seem to get the impression from my students that this is uncharted territory. This is a brand new experience, and they're seeing something for the first time — and for a lot of our students, they don't have much to compare it to. No matter what their experience is."

"We can't put ourselves in our students' shoes [because] we don't know what it's like to show up and not have some information you need and then have to go around and ask questions."

Often community college faculty members who have experienced the entering student process with their own children or have enrolled in classes themselves at the college report that everything they have heard from their students about the process is accurate. Even knowing all they know about the college, they say the process "can be a very daunting and unpleasant experience."

Financial Aid

Three-fourths of entering students responding to *SENSE* say they applied for financial assistance to attend college. Almost 60% say they applied one month or more before classes started. Less than half indicate that they received funds before the beginning of the term. Further, less than half (49%) agree that the college provided them with adequate information about financial assistance, including available scholarships, loans, and grants. Little more than one-third (34%) say a college staff member helped determine whether they qualified for financial assistance. While three-fourths of entering students say they were aware that the college offered financial aid advising, more than half say they did not use the service.

When students describe their experiences during registration, they typically offer negative comments about the financial aid process. They talk about cumbersome procedures, long waits, and confusion about the steps they need to take and the information they need to provide. Generally, those students who report having an easier time with financial aid say they filled out the Free Application for Federal Student Aid (FAFSA) form while still in high school:

"The financial aid is very, very, very unorganized."

"I just finished applying for next semester, for spring, and it was a chore trying to figure everything out, what went where. And I had turned everything in, [but] I got an email back saying, 'You still missed these things,' and I had no idea that I needed them, and the deadline was coming up, so it was really hard to know these things. 'Cause I went to the financial aid advisor, I went and I talked to her, she helped me out, but apparently I didn't get all the information that I needed, and so I got the email and had to very quickly get everything together to turn it in. That wasn't helpful."

"When I got accepted for financial aid, they never told me that you had to get a degree plan. So every time I went up there, I [was told I] was accepted, but they never gave me the money. So then one day I just kept going, kept going, I guess they got tired of me going, and they told me I had to get a degree plan. So then that's how I got the money."

"I kept coming back because they never gave me the money. And after waiting a month or two, I finally came in on the very last day; if I hadn't walked in sometime last week, I wouldn't have gotten my loans. But every time I came back, they said, 'Oh, you'll get an email eventually,' and I never did."

"[A] big thing is understanding how financial aid works when you actually receive it. I applied in July, and I still [in September] haven't received it. I'm about 600 dollars into classes. I want to know if I'm getting refunded for that. Is that coming in to my financial aid? It's a lot of stuff they're really vague about unless you personally go out and go do your homework and try to find out. If they put out the effort, we wouldn't be stuck in these situations."

"I've been applying, I've been doing everything, and they never answer me. I always have a little flag next to my parents' signature. If they don't want to approve it, just tell me, 'I'm not gonna approve it.' But I'm constantly signing, going there."

"You want us to go to school, you want us to have an education? Well, you turn us down by how long we have to wait on the line. Yes, we have to wait for things in our life, we understand that, but it's way too long, the lines."

Students readily acknowledge that they need more help understanding the financial aid process and completing all the paperwork that is required:

"Most of the time they'll just say, 'Well, pick up this pamphlet and read this booklet, fill out the information, and go here, do this,' but they don't tell you what you're giving them, they don't tell you why you're doing it. And most of the time, if you try to ask them, they'll say, 'If there's anything you don't understand, why don't you read it all first and then if there's anything you don't understand, come back and we'll answer your questions for you.' But that can be even more inconvenient than if they would just go over it with you at the same time as you get the information in the first place."

"Just because you look at the form does not mean that every question is going to be answered within that form, or it may be in a term that the new student may not be able to understand."

Now and then, students in a community college report that the financial aid process went smoothly for them, and they point to the helpfulness of staff members who worked with them:

"They explain [financial aid] to you right away — if you need it, think you need it, they'll try to get it for you. Even if you don't need it, if you qualify for it, it's there for you."

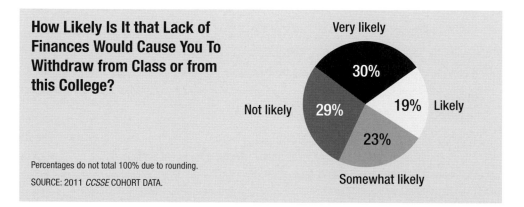

How Likely Is It that Lack of Finances Would Cause You To Withdraw from Class or from this College?

Very likely 30%
Likely 19%
Somewhat likely 23%
Not likely 29%

Percentages do not total 100% due to rounding.
SOURCE: 2011 *CCSSE* COHORT DATA.

On *CCSSE*, students are asked how likely it is that any of several factors would result in their withdrawing from a class or the college — a lack of financial resources, working full-time, caring for dependents, or being academically unprepared. More than 70% of students say a lack of resources could cause them to withdraw. In focus groups, students frequently say they are attending a community college because it costs less than attending a four-year institution. Students are clear about the urgency of their financial needs: "They want you to wait for next year, next year; no, we need the money now to start school now. Please help us." *Are we listening?*

Assessment and Placement

On *SENSE,* most entering students (87%) indicate that they were required to take a placement test at their community college before they could enroll in courses. Seventy-three percent report that they were required to enroll in the courses indicated by their placement test scores. Some students report that they were surprised to learn that they had to take a placement test, and they often say they did not understand before they took the test that their scores on the test would dictate the classes they could take:

> *"When I first took it, I kind of was bummed out because I tested at the bottom English, bottom math, thinking, wow, I gotta start at the bottom. But then once I did it and realized that this is a step-by-step process, I was so grateful that they had that testing, that they put me where I needed to be, because everything was for a reason. I didn't see it at first, but the second semester I started to understand the reasoning behind it, and now I'm very grateful that the placement test was there."*

After taking the test, some students report that they met with an advisor to get the results of their placement tests and, based on their test scores, that individual told them what classes they needed to take. Others say they did not meet with anyone:

> *"My best friend told me what I needed to do. I took my placement test and never saw an advisor after that. My mom enrolled me online so I was already all enrolled. I just had to take my placement test, and then I had to sign up for my classes online, and I had a sheet of the classes I needed to take, and my friend just helped me sign up for all of them. I never had the need to go to [an advisor]."*

> *"I have no idea why I got placed where I was."*

Usually students report that no one offered them an opportunity to review for the test, and some say they learned too late that they could have prepared for it. Among those who participated in a review session, opinions about the usefulness of the session are mixed. Some say they found the review to be helpful; some say they were surprised when they saw that the test had very few questions and little margin for error:

> *"We took a five-hour review session. It helped a little."*

"I didn't even know they had [a review]."

"[I learned about the review] through my mom. She used to take classes here just to finish up her associate [degree]. And she knew that they would have review sessions for people who were about to take the placement tests. They would do it all summer long. I think every month. It was on like a Sunday. I learned through her."

Some students say when they came to campus to register for classes, they were told about the placement test, were given a website address, and were told they could review for the placement test online. Some say they checked it out but would have needed some guidance in using the web-based tools. Others say they did not look at the recommended website:

"The teacher at the [college] that helped us and everything, she had given me stuff to study. I think she had pulled it from the website that they have. I didn't study it, but she said that she got it off the website so I guess it was there, but for the other people, they weren't told about it."

In general, students' comments reflect uncertainty about whether there are opportunities to prepare for the placement test and also raise questions about whether there is any value in trying to prepare. Having experienced the process, however, they do suggest that new students try to get ready before they take the placement test but also try not to be intimidated by the whole process.

"Be prepared for the COMPASS test; there isn't much you can study for, but you can study a little bit. Just hold your head high and see what you can do."

Advising

Students who meet with an advisor before they start classes at the community college often say the advising process fell short of what they needed and had hoped for. On the *SENSE* survey, 70% of students report that an advisor helped them pick classes, yet only 39% say an advisor helped them set academic goals and create a plan for achieving them:

"After you do your placement testing, you go meet with an advisor to pick out your classes and see what classes you need, but my advisor wasn't really helpful. She kind of said, 'Here are the classes you need and go make your schedule.' I had a whole bunch of questions for her, and she said I'd have to come back."

"My counselor said, 'I'd like to discuss this with you, but I have someone else after you. We should finish this up as soon as possible.'"

"I feel like I'm wasting time because counselors just write down the classes you need and give you the paper."

"Unfortunately, they weren't as much help as I would hope. I mean, they registered me for the classes, but they didn't really give me a direction that maybe I could go in. They just signed me up for in-general courses. He didn't talk to me … about making a plan. That was a personal choice. He just did what I asked and sent me home."

"When you go in there they're just gonna do the basics, like set you up with the basic classes, but they're not gonna show you, 'Oh, you need to take these classes to get toward your major.' Then you might end up scheduling classes that you don't necessarily need, and then that's wasting your time as well. But a closed mouth don't get fed. If you don't say anything, then they won't necessarily give you that information. You gotta fish for it; it isn't like they just easily give it to you."

"Just with the experiences I've had, it's pretty much like, 'Oh, what's your schedule? Okay, you want to take this? Okay, we'll schedule you this class at this time so you can do this.' And there's still the matter of 'do I want to take this class right now? Is it going to be right for me to take right now? What prerequisites am I gonna need?'"

In addition to wanting help in setting goals and charting their course at the college, students retrospectively say that they had a serious need for someone to help them make good decisions about how to balance classes, study time, and their other responsibilities to jobs, family, and community. On the *SENSE* survey, only 26% of entering students say someone talked with them about what's going on in their lives and the implications for how many classes to take during their first term:

"So for a first-time person going to community college — you know that you have X amount of time, and you haven't really studied to find out how much time you're gonna need to do your classes or to do your studies or your homework. Then you're lost, really, when you go in, and that's what happened to me. I went in and I knew the approach that I wanted, I knew what I wanted to go after, and so I went after that. But nobody said, 'What about your job? What about your home? What about your children? What about the time you need to spend with your wife? What about church?' And so now I have a schedule that I have to put all of that to the side so that I can focus only on schoolwork. And so it's schoolwork, bed, schoolwork, bed, schoolwork, bed."

"[In] my English class, I'm doing great, but [in] my math class, I am not doing well at all. And I think I took on too much at one time. My time is allotted for maybe two classes, but I took on three classes. And not ever going to school before, I went and did something that I really should've got a lot of counsel on. And so I jumped and said, 'Yeah, I can do this and I can do that and, oh, yeah, take a psychology class, too.' And so I took math, English, psychology, and now I am catching it."

Those who report having a positive experience with an advisor as they entered college are specific about what made it helpful to them:

"Well, she sat down with me and told me what to expect with nursing and made sure that that was the field that I was sure I wanted to go into. And she helped me set up all of my classes. It was really good; she was really thorough, and she was great."

"They asked what major you wanted to go for, and they basically showed me a little plan, like all the classes I needed."

"I told him my goal at the end, and [he told me] what classes I should take for my undergrad before I even go for my [transfer] school, and I think that's so, so important. Because the schools I'm looking into now to transfer to, I have to see what classes I need to take to get to where I need to go. And I believe, for me anyway, if I didn't sit down and take that time, what's the point? I'd be taking classes that would be irrelevant; I wouldn't use any of the credits. I mean it's always good to learn, but when we have a goal, it's like, what progress am I making toward that goal?"

Entering Students *Agree* or *Strongly Agree* that:

Percentage	Statement
70%	An advisor helped me identify the courses I needed to take during my first term.
60%	An advisor helped me select a course of study, program, or major.
39%	An advisor helped me set academic goals and create a plan for achieving them.
26%	A college staff member talked with me about my commitments outside of school to help me figure out how many courses to take.

0%   20%   40%   60%   80%   100%

SOURCE: 2011 *SENSE* COHORT DATA.

What's My Major?

Fewer than half of entering students report on the *SENSE* survey that they knew the college offered career counseling services, and more than 80% of students say during their fourth or fifth week of college that they have not yet seen a career counselor. Yet in focus groups, even later in the academic year, students say they want more help with career counseling and do not feel like they receive much support in that area. "People are always trying to stress with us that we need to choose a major, but they don't really help us with it." Rather than meeting with a different counselor for this support, students are instead looking for more career-related conversations with the advisor who helps them choose classes:

"I think the counselors should be there to be able to tell you not just what the degrees are, because I can read in the book what the degree is. What I want to know is what the degree entails, what kind of jobs you can get with that degree."

Emerging research shows that community college students are more likely to achieve their goals if they enter a major concentration or coherent program of study. A recent study by Davis Jenkins and Sung-Woo Cho concluded that students entering a program of study in their first year achieved substantially better academic outcomes than students who did not enter a concentration until their second year or later. Specifically, they found that "more than half of the students who first entered a program of study in their first year earned a certificate or associate degree, transferred to a four-year institution (either with or without a credential), or earned a bachelor's degree from an outside institution."[1]

Yet more than half of students 26 years of age or younger who indicate their intent to pursue a degree or certificate when they enter college never succeed in determining their field of study. College leaders should consider that simply helping younger students declare a major or identify an area of concentration might result in increased college completion rates.[2]

On *CCSSE*, when asked about the importance of various college services, students consistently point to academic advising and planning as the most important college support service. In focus groups, students do not hesitate to suggest that all students should be required to meet with an advisor:

"When new students first come in, I think they should have a mandatory one-on-one sit down with a counselor to really discuss in detail their degree plan and stuff."

"I think it should be mandatory that every student has an advisor. I think it would be good if everyone had somebody they could talk to that is school-related and can help you in your personal and your educational life."

"I've had many times where I've had to make the decision between quitting school and getting another job or taking out another loan and keep being on at school. And I guess part of it is that I'm very stubborn, and the other part is I have very good academic advisors."

Hearing this from students, college leaders often worry that the institution cannot afford to hire the multitude of new advisors that they assume would be required to meet the expressed need. However, a growing number of colleges are implementing group advising (including academic planning, goal setting, and time management skill building), often incorporated into a student success class, orientation, or first-year seminar. In that way, the students benefit from engagement with other students as well as with the advisor, and the experience becomes a routine (*not optional!*) part of their educational pathway.

Students Offer Advice

- Provide a checklist outlining the enrollment process steps and deadlines.

- Streamline the financial aid process.

- Make advising mandatory.

- Assign an advisor to each student. "They know you and know what you're doing, know what problems you're having."

Carly's Story

Carly had dreams of going to college. She was a straight-A student and contender for class valedictorian. Despite a troubled home life, she was about to become the first person in her family to graduate from high school. "School was kind of my escape from reality," she says.

When she became pregnant at age 17, she graduated early and put her college dreams on hold. Carly spent the next several years as a single mother raising her son, got married, and then at age 23, a few weeks after giving birth to twin girls, she enrolled at a community college.

GETTING STARTED: Carly had no idea how to choose a major, much less how to translate a major into a job. "It's not because I'm not smart or not good at anything. It's just because I don't know what's out there," she said. She sought counseling, but she came away disappointed. "They thought that I knew what I wanted to be. I would always tell them, 'I don't have any idea what I want to be and that's … why I waited so many years to go to school.'"

CHALLENGES: Carly placed into developmental math, and the college required her to enroll in a college success class. Although she says she needed the math refresher, she found the pace of the class painfully slow. "Once I have it in my head, I pretty much know it. And the other two hours of the class I'm bored," she says. She had the option to test out, but she did not see that as a good move. "[I'm] not a genius, I don't claim to know everything. If you test out, then there's a chance that something vital is gonna be missing from what you learned that you're gonna need in a later class," she says.

Her student success class was better. There she found a professor who "actually tries to understand what I'm telling him" when she peppered him with questions to help her find a major. He recommended a website; still, nothing clicked.

Near the end of her first semester, a counselor pointed Carly toward a major that seemed to make sense: nuclear operations. With a new plant nearby, jobs seemed assured. She signed on, explaining, "It's where the money is, and we have lots of kids, so we need the money." But her choice was short-lived; she took one class, dropped it, and "… decided I was in no way, shape, or form interested in this." Carly switched her major back to Undecided. "I'll figure it out on my own," she thought.

FINDING WHAT WORKS: The next fall, Carly enrolled in a psychology class. Soon, she recalls, "I was really hooked, and I went to the counseling office to ask what kind of degrees you can get with it. This time, a new counselor actually tried to point me in the direction my mind wants to go," suggesting a career in child psychology.

NEXT STEPS: Carly plans to transfer to a university to earn both a teaching certificate and a degree in psychology. Trying to manage her young family, she switched to online classes, but she misses everything about being in the classroom. "'Hate' is a strong word, but I hate doing classes online," she says. "I like having someone who is right there if I have a question when I'm reading or … trying to figure something out. You can't do that online."

OBSERVATIONS: Carly recognizes that taking time to find a major is normal. "I figured it out as I went through," she says. "You have to learn who you are. You're still growing and you just have to expect to have to change …. It would have been nice if I heard something like that when I was starting."

Pauline's Story

When Pauline finished high school 20 years ago, college was the last thing on her mind. At age 17, she had a new baby and was moving to a new city. "It was just really hard for me to focus on anything except for my child," she says. "I wish, though, that someone [had] pushed me to go to college. I think even at 17, 18 years old, you still need that push to … set your goals and achieve things. If someone stepped in, I think I would have gotten into [college] a lot quicker."

Finally, with her three children out of high school and a supportive second husband, Pauline enrolled in a community college.

GETTING STARTED: Balancing family life with a part-time waitressing job, Pauline began slowly. "I started part-time so that would give me a better feel of what I was getting myself into," she says. "Because I'm older, I knew that I needed to understand how college classes work first, before I got myself into a big mess."

CHALLENGES: Pauline went to the advising center, but she says that her first two advisors did little more than show her how to physically register for classes she already had selected. "That's the thing, they don't advise. You go in there and they're like, 'What is it you want to take?' instead of looking at your background and seeing if maybe they can help you see if it's something that you like to do," she says. "Students overwhelm themselves — they need to be told, 'If you take a bunch of challenging courses, then you're gonna be straining yourself just to pass.'"

Rusty from years away from academics, Pauline indeed strained, but she still did not pass her first math class. "It was too challenging …" she says. "I was taking all these classes — algebra and everything that I was totally lost in. It lowered my spirits."

Even with improved study skills, Pauline still finds college challenging. While willing to seek help when she needs it, Pauline describes the college's tutoring services as overtaxed. "Sometimes they have only two people helping 15 or 20 students. There's many times that I've gone … and waited and waited and not gotten any help and had to leave just because I had to go to class."

FINDING WHAT WORKS: Persisting in her quest for advising, Pauline found a new counselor who helped her create a program plan. "She was really interested in what I had to say and in getting me on the right path," she says. The counselor guided Pauline to a student success course, where she learned how to keep tabs on her progress and to manage her time. "You learn to put priorities where they need to be," Pauline says. "Now if I want to get through a course, I know I'm going to have to focus … ."

That course led Pauline to the career center, where advisors assessed how well her aptitudes fit with her chosen career. She found the services helpful but wishes she had discovered them earlier. That's also true of the student success course. "I think it should be mandatory," Pauline says.

NEXT STEPS: Pauline plans to find a job in medical transcription to help support her family while she continues to work toward a management degree and her dream of owning a business. "What keeps me going is that I've set my goal and I keep picturing my future," she says. "If I don't do this, if I just give up, I'm not only not setting a good example for my kids, I'm also not succeeding for myself."

CHAPTER 5

Learning How To Succeed in College

The two primary opportunities community colleges offer for students to acclimate to the college environment are orientation and student success courses. Less frequently offered is participation in a first-semester learning community or a structured first-year experience or seminar. The key word is "offer." On *SENSE,* fewer than half of entering community college students report that they participated in an on-campus orientation, and only 27% report that they enrolled in a course specifically designed to teach skills and strategies to help them succeed in college. By contrast, as shown in preliminary results from the Center's Community College Institutional Survey (CCIS), out of 288 responding colleges, 96% report that they offer orientation, and 83% offer a student success course.

While students who took part in a well-designed orientation or enrolled in a student success course typically describe how the experiences helped them adjust to college, faculty and staff in many institutions still argue about whether it is appropriate or desirable to require either for new students. In fact, 2011 CCIS results indicate that among colleges that offer these experiences, only 38% (105 of 276 colleges) require orientation for all first-time students, and approximately 15% (35 out of 238 colleges) require first-time students to enroll in a student success course. The questions college leaders must consider are: *Are we doing all we can to equip students with the tools and skills requisite to their success in college? Are we, in fact, setting students up for failure if we do not provide the on-ramp to college that they clearly need?*

College Orientation

Many community colleges offer some sort of orientation for incoming freshmen. Some offer an online orientation that students can access at any time, others offer voluntary orientation sessions on campus, and some do both.

At many colleges, faculty and staff suggest that their busy new students will rebel against a requirement to attend orientation and will walk away from the college if a mandatory orientation policy is put in place. Perhaps as a middle-ground solution, leaders at a number of community colleges are deciding that a preferred alternative is to require an online-only orientation, in the belief that students will find it more convenient and that younger students in particular will prefer the online environment. Some colleges reinforce the requirement by blocking students' registration until the online orientation is completed.

Interestingly, in workshops and focus groups with college faculty and staff, almost all who attended four-year institutions report participating in a freshman orientation on campus. When asked why they participated, almost all say, "It was required." When asked if the orientation was helpful to them, they inevitably respond, "Yes." They talk about how the experience helped to calm their fears about college and helped them learn what would be expected of them in college. They add that they appreciated having the opportunity to meet faculty and other students before classes began.

Do we assume that community college students need less orientation than those attending four-year institutions? Do we believe that community college students deserve less opportunity to gain the knowledge they need to successfully begin college?

According to results from *SENSE,* only slightly more than 11% of entering students participate in online orientation prior to the beginning of class and, as noted above, fewer than half participate in an on-campus orientation prior to the beginning of class. Eighteen percent indicate that they were unaware of an orientation at their college, and more than 20% of student respondents say they were unable to participate in orientation due to scheduling or other issues. Far more of the younger community college students — those 18–24 years old — say they attended an on-campus orientation than do older students (48% vs. 36%).

Community college students disagree with college leaders' assumptions about their resistance to a required orientation. A few weeks into their first term,

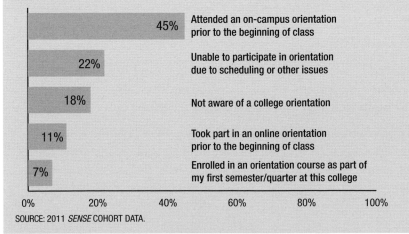

Entering Students Report on Their Experience with the College's New Student Orientation:

- 45% Attended an on-campus orientation prior to the beginning of class
- 22% Unable to participate in orientation due to scheduling or other issues
- 18% Not aware of a college orientation
- 11% Took part in an online orientation prior to the beginning of class
- 7% Enrolled in an orientation course as part of my first semester/quarter at this college

0%   20%   40%   60%   80%   100%

SOURCE: 2011 *SENSE* COHORT DATA.

students participating in focus groups have a lot to say about their need for an orientation and the components that should be part of that experience.

Furthermore, in focus groups at colleges that require students to complete an online orientation before registering for classes, students demonstrate with index fingers on an imaginary computer keyboard how they rather mindlessly meet the requirement: "click, click, click, submit." Asked what they have learned from the online session, they smile and shake their heads. "Really didn't pay much attention," someone often reports, and others agree.

Is Orientation Required, or Isn't It?

Students often say that the college is unclear about whether they are required to attend orientation or even whether there is an orientation at all. Sometimes students are aware of orientation; sometimes they are not. Sometimes they go; sometimes they do not. Sometimes they hear that orientation is required and still do not go. Sometimes they are not sure what they are supposed to take away from the experience. And sometimes they do not even realize that the session they attended was an orientation:

"I think they have some sort of orientation here; like I said, I didn't really go."

"You're supposed to attend the first-time-in-college orientation and, if not, then … next semester or next year when you're here again, you'll have to attend it. So you're supposed to. It's really good that you walk around the campus and that they talk to you, and I did it."

"They just went over a lot of stuff about not dropping classes. If you drop more than six classes, then you're in some sort of trouble. I don't know. But I got there kind of late so I didn't get to do the whole walking around the school and everything. So I'm gonna have to do that by myself."

"I came in to register, and the person I was supposed to talk to wasn't there, but somebody just brought me up to a room where they were having an orientation … I wasn't paying attention too much. She was just going over the PowerPoint. It was a lot of stuff I had heard in high school."

"We had orientation. It was a bunch of new people who [were] just coming to the campus, and they set us down and gave us little notebooks, books, stuff like that. Talk to us. We got an advisor."

"I didn't know that was the orientation. I thought it would be like a whole bunch of people. It was like six of us. All right, I did orientation."

"When I was there, I was kind of confused on everything. I ain't gonna lie to you. I just ended up sitting in a room, and then she just started giving people papers.

I'm like, 'Where am I at?' And they said, 'You're in orientation.' Oh, I accidentally fell into orientation. So I got that out of the way on accident. But I'm glad I did it because I learned a lot of stuff I did not know and as soon as I walked out of orientation, I knew exactly what I needed to go do."

In those instances when the college had been clear about inviting students to a scheduled and well-organized orientation and students attended the session, many say they found it to be helpful:

"They had an orientation day, and I went to it. I think there was like two of them — one of them in August, and I went to that one. It was a room and they had an instructor who had a video, so of course they showed about campus life and whatever and we viewed it. And in front of us we had computers, and he was directing us what to pick, so I got to pick my classes. But if I didn't understand what I was doing, they had other individuals who would help you."

"I think it was good — the information they gave us about financial aid, about expectations, study hints, stuff like that. And then they had the little things outside, the booths, for the extra stuff that you can do like the intramurals and all that. So I thought it was useful."

"They just pretty much showed you around. They introduced a couple of teachers and then sort of suggested how you were gonna be treated in the college by a lot of the professors."

"It was exciting, it was fun. I was like, 'Orientation, hey, I'm almost there, I'm almost there.'"

Despite a belief expressed by faculty and staff in many colleges that students will welcome the convenience of online orientation, students typically say they prefer attending an orientation session on campus — citing once again the value they place on personal connections:

"We think [it] would help out the students [if] there would be a more personal orientation with [a] tour. The options they give you are take personal orientation or do an online orientation. I can understand how it would be more convenient sometimes to take an online orientation, but really, have a more personal orientation with the tours [so] that you can understand where the buildings are, what the lettering system is, and how the college works in general."

Early in their first term, many students understand retrospectively that they needed more guidance as they started college. Whether or not they were aware that the college offered an orientation during the registration period, they did not necessarily understand the value of attending at that time. A few weeks later, asked in focus groups to recommend features of an ideal college, they do not hesitate to advise colleges to require an orientation:

"We said orientation should be required, so that way people can get a better understanding of what their classes are, and the first time they're out here they won't have to look for this classroom."

"We said mandatory orientation."

"A lot of us are a little upset about the orientation, that we didn't have to go to the Boot Camp for first-year students. So they should've maybe kind of advertised it a little bit more. Class explanations. Basically you can look in the catalog and get a description of the courses, but what we want is to maybe meet a professor or someone in that specific area, to kind of explain or ... be there at registration."

In summary, students' views on college orientation warrant emphasis: They repeatedly say that orientation is important, that they benefit from a personalized orientation experience, and that colleges should make it mandatory for all entering students. New students' clearly expressed views about their needs and what will help them in a face-to-face orientation session bring an obligation to colleges that orientation be required, immediately relevant, substantive, and engaging for students. Students understand that. *Are we listening?*

Student Success Courses

Student success courses are intended to help students build knowledge and skills essential for success in college. Typically, the course includes a focus on study skills, time-management skills, note-taking skills, and test-taking skills and provide guidance for students in using the information and academic support resources available at the college. Often, academic goal setting and planning are part of the course as well.

In some community colleges, the course is required for certain targeted groups of students, such as those testing into developmental courses; in other colleges, the course is simply recommended for these students. In some colleges, the course is required for all first-time-in-college students or those who have earned less than a specified number of college credits; in other colleges, the course is simply recommended for those students.

The course takes many forms — sometimes it is designed as a stand-alone class, sometimes the course is integrated into a learning community, sometimes the course is compressed into the first weeks of the academic term, and sometimes it is a semester-long or quarter-long experience. In some colleges, the course is designed as a credit-bearing class and is transferrable; in others, it is not. Individual colleges give the course a variety of names, such as Learning Frameworks, Freshman Seminar, Student Life Skills, College Success Course, Extended Orientation, and Student Development.

Responding to questions about their experiences in student success courses, many students in focus groups indicate that the course helped them develop skills to become a better student, such as study skills, time-management skills, note-taking skills, and test-taking skills. Students also report that the course helped them learn about college services and policies.

In focus groups at the beginning of their first academic term, students often are less than enthusiastic about having to take a college success course and are concerned that it will be a waste of their time and money because they believe they already know what the course is designed to teach them. And indeed, for some, their fears are realized. Their comments raise important considerations for colleges about course content and the timing of content, in terms of when students need to know certain things — prior to the beginning of classes, very early in the first term, or by the end of that first semester or quarter. As a student at one college describes her class:

> *"It was the most pointless thing I've ever had to sit through. I guess it would have been valuable if I'd had it before I started school. They told us how the bookstore and everything worked. They told us how to check our email! You have to know that stuff before you start classes. They did focus a lot on study skills. That was the most, I guess, you could take from that class."*

Despite their earlier concerns, a few weeks into the college success class, students typically report that the class is useful:

> *"I think it is [useful] now. Before, I told you I thought that the class was going to be stupid, but I like it."*

> *"Some days it's kind of like, yeah, I already knew that and it's kind of like refreshing you, and you're like, 'all right I can do that,' you know, 'instead of doing this.' But my teacher is really awesome. He has it up on a slide show, and it just kind of goes with you and shows us all these different ways. It teaches you what kind of learner you are and stuff like that. And he has all these different activities to get you to think about it in different ways. It kind of gets your wheels turning, like 'oh, all right,' instead of just writing it down, you can do it this way or just different things. I like it."*

Even when students are concerned about whether they really need to learn what the college success course offers, they quickly decide that the class still has value to them: "The plus side of that class, though, even if you think it's a waste of time, that class goes toward your GPA so it's an easy A, it's an easy high grade." Arguably, if an "easy A" represents an individual having learned how to be an effective college student, everyone wins.

Students are consistent in their comments about how such courses help them:

"Freshman Seminar is good for that because it gives you test-taking strategies, study skills, managing time, money — gives you a structured idea of getting organized."

"It was just like teaching you about college. You got your student ID. We would walk around the campus."

"It just teaches you time management and setting your goals, like what you want to do further in your education."

"Right now he's teaching us how to take notes in a way that later on we can still be able to read them and go back to them as ways to study and stuff. But it's supposed to be to help you learn how to study, learn how to take notes, learn just basically how to be in college."

"I like it a lot. It's really useful. Just like they have been saying, they teach you how to take good notes, how to study, how to manage your time, just everything that you need to know to be successful in college. It's a really cool class. I enjoy it."

"Mine was a six-week [class], so it ended last week, but it was actually really useful. She gave us a scavenger hunt, and you had to go around, and one group went to financial aid and then presented all the information, and one went to the tutoring center. All the services the school has, that's actually how I kind of learned the most about them was through that class."

"I was told it was an easy grade, and, since I've never been to college before, I figured it could be helpful so I took the class, like study skills, writing, getting research. It's everything built into one class. It's helpful. It is."

Is the College Success Course Mandatory, or Isn't It?

Students frequently are confused about whether the course is mandatory at their college. Some students report learning from a counselor or other students that the course is required. Later they find out that other students did not have to take it. Some students hear about the course from others after the term has started, and they are annoyed that they did not hear about it before.

If a college mandates participation for some students and not for others, those distinctions typically are not clear to students, as the following focus group conversation demonstrates:

"The college success class — I heard it was mandatory [for] all new students."

"I also heard it was mandatory, and then I heard a lot of people weren't taking it."

"That's what confuses me, though. All the people are telling me that this class is required. I didn't even hear about this class 'til two weeks into the semester. What is triple A 15? Oh, that's the success for student class. I was like, that exists?"

"Same here."

"You take it, [they] teach you time-management skills, once a week. And it's required? Yeah. Why didn't my advisor tell me about it? I don't know."

"College is different than high school. You have to manage your time different. I'm barely starting to get a hold of that. I never even knew about that class."

"I was told about it and that it was mandatory … but I didn't end up taking it anyways. It wasn't obviously that required 'cause I know a lot of other students that aren't taking it also."

Data from colleges requiring all incoming students or targeted groups of students to enroll in a student success course in the first term are strongly encouraging. Through their own evaluations, colleges are finding that students who complete a student success course are more likely than previous cohorts or non-participating peers to succeed on a number of indicators: semester completion, successful course completion, persistence into the next term, and so on.

Students who have the opportunity to experience well-executed orientation and student success courses understand their benefits. And many students who miss out on those experiences lament that lost opportunity. *How can colleges make it inescapable that more students have the intentionally designed experiences that help them learn how to succeed in college?*

Mercedes' Story

Despite the odds stacked against her, Mercedes is now studying kinesiology/sports medicine at her "dream" university. She came from a neighborhood with "low-to-no expectations," but she turned things around for herself through her passion for sports. "From then on out, I liked passing my classes because I liked playing sports and I like doing well so that I could have a reward for myself, which was running at a track meet," she says.

With test scores too low for university admission, Mercedes enrolled in a community college. She had difficulties, but she says the experience was for the best: "Without that experience, I wouldn't have known how hard it was gonna be. If I had come [to the university] first, I think I would have gotten more involved with the whole college life [rather] than my academics … I wouldn't have known how to approach things or who to talk to. Without community college, it would have really destroyed ever being here now."

GETTING STARTED: Trying to escape her neighborhood, Mercedes chose a community college across town. "I knew that negative energy or being around the same people wasn't gonna be any better for me," she says. She then landed a job in the college admissions office. "I loved the atmosphere," Mercedes says. "I was ready to start school. I was *so* ready." She attended orientation and found it "really useful."

CHALLENGES: Mercedes felt confident that she would breeze through her classes and was disappointed when she tested into remedial math. "You're gonna pay for a class you're not getting credit for. Just hearing that, it's not a good feeling," she says. She did not learn until much later about the fast-track option at her college, in which two developmental courses are packed into one semester.

Although she says she was bored with some classes that were too easy, Mercedes found others to be more challenging. She tried tutoring for some classes, but she did not think she needed help in others and didn't want to seem "high maintenance."

Recognizing that she was underprepared for college and had no idea how to study effectively, Mercedes found it hard to balance school and work. "Everything came at me so fast, and I couldn't handle it …. I never experienced having to go through all this stress … ." she says. "I'd procrastinate way too much — I could do that in high school, I could pull it off. But in college, I just could not do it."

"I was not studying enough, not devoting enough time, not taking the initiative to talk to my professor or get with people in my class, make groups — study groups, things like that," Mercedes recalls. "I didn't take advantage of any of that."

FINDING WHAT WORKS: Through conversations with co-workers in the admissions office, Mercedes learned that she could begin classes at a nearby university and work toward her bachelor's degree while completing her associate degree. She currently is attending the university and taking a class to improve her study skills.

OBSERVATIONS: A little distance has given Mercedes the ability to look back and see things more clearly: "I was the one who had questions, and people would look at me funny like, 'Well, like, don't you get it?' And I really didn't. Now I can finally admit it was hard."

Nadia's Story

Nadia is proof that timing can have a major impact on college success. The 32-year-old student soon will graduate with an associate degree and plans to continue her education. She made a few attempts at college when she was younger, but she never finished. "I had to work full-time to support myself, and I was very young," she says. "I had a busy social life, and my priorities were different. I didn't have the drive. School was obviously not number one for me."

Born and raised in Iran, Nadia came to the United States in 2000 and worked a variety of jobs before attempting college again at age 30. "Most of my family is college educated," she says. "I know the value of that. I realized I have a lot of potential, and I'm smart. I have a lot to offer. If I ever want to live up to that, then I need education and direction. And I knew that education was what was going to give me direction in life."

GETTING STARTED: Nadia enrolled in a community college. "After 12 years of a break, I wasn't sure if I could do it. I wasn't confident enough [to go to a university]," she says. "I needed to ease my way in, and I thought community college would allow me to do that. Community college grants you the luxury of time — you can take your time and figure out what you want to do." She worked closely with an advisor who is a specialist for transfer students. "I did not waste time and money because I knew what classes I needed to take," she says.

FINDING WHAT WORKS: "Every teacher I've had is in love with their job. I have had very positive experiences," she says.

Even when she had to take remedial courses, Nadia stayed positive. "I didn't mind it at all. I have to learn what I have to learn, right?" she says. "The classes helped prepare me. You cannot jump on top of the ladder — you have to go step-by-step."

A job as a student ambassador for the college enhanced Nadia's experience. "I am meeting a lot of people I would never otherwise meet," she says. "I'm exposed to a new phase of education by simply working on campus."

Nadia earned a 4.0 GPA in her first quarter. She attributes some of her success to her own hard work: "I showed up for class, participated in class discussions, and I read the assignments. I kept on top of everything and never fell behind," she says. "I put school before everything, except for family."

She also recognizes the important role of college resources such as instructors' office hours, advisors, and tutors. "You have to find the help, acknowledge when you need something, and find out what resources there are," she says. "You miss out on a lot if you don't ask for help."

NEXT STEPS: After earning her associate degree, Nadia plans to transfer and earn a bachelor's degree in social psychology. "I'm convinced I'm prepared for what's next," she says. "I am in touch with an advisor at the university who says I am a very competitive applicant. She can see that I have received a quality education that has groomed me for that next adventure." Further goals include earning a master's degree and a career working in higher education. "There is a teacher in me, but I'm not necessarily going for a teaching degree," Nadia says. "I'm very open to what life has for me."

CHAPTER 6

Engaging in Learning: What Matters?

"The atmosphere's just great, everybody knows what's going on and everybody's interested and everybody's active, and the teacher is treating us like it's not just another lecture — it's actually class, and you can make it fun."

— Community college student

For many community college students, the time they spend in class, whether it is on campus or online, is the only time they connect to their instructors, their peers, and the resources and services the college offers. Balancing their studies with work and family, they very often spend whatever time is necessary to attend classes and then move on to other commitments. When students first enroll in the community college, many explicitly say that is their intention — to come to class, then leave.

Research and practice show that when colleges create engaging learning experiences for students and make many of those experiences inescapable, community college students respond positively, connecting to the college and their learning in ways they might not have anticipated. And those experiences must occur from the moment students begin their first classes. Unfortunately, findings from the *SENSE* survey show many students are not getting early opportunities in their classes to benefit from engaging instructional strategies.

There is considerable consensus about what constitutes effective educational practice in undergraduate education. Active and collaborative learning, intensive student-faculty and student-student interaction, frequent feedback, and high expectations accompanied by high support figure strongly in that consensus. Students clearly articulate those practices when they describe the types of classes and the qualities of instructors that engage and motivate them.

When faculty members reflect on their teaching experiences and the "best classes" they have taught, most identify the same characteristics that students describe. Some say they did not start out teaching in the most engaging way but are learning as they go. One instructor acknowledges, for example, that she changed her approach "because I remember my first day I did it the way I was taught — and I turned around, and half my class was gone, and the other half was asleep."

When talking about their best experiences — and their worst experiences — in community college classes, students describe the culture of the class, what is happening in the class, the way their instructors work with them, and how they are challenged to become better students. And they single out those elements that either make it difficult for them to engage or make it exciting for them to be in the class. They also talk about what is happening in the class or required by the instructor that encourages them to continue their learning outside of class sessions.

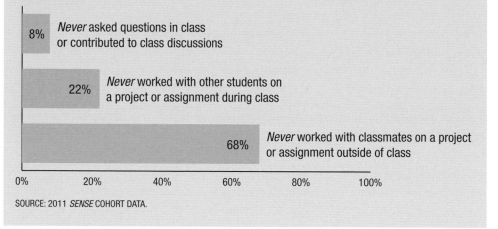

Entering Students Report that During the First Three Weeks of Class, They:

- 8% *Never* asked questions in class or contributed to class discussions
- 22% *Never* worked with other students on a project or assignment during class
- 68% *Never* worked with classmates on a project or assignment outside of class

SOURCE: 2011 *SENSE* COHORT DATA.

Clear Expectations

Most students responding to *SENSE* indicate that instructors clearly explained the syllabus (91% *agree* or *strongly agree*) and course grading policies (88% *agree* or *strongly agree*).

In focus groups, students who recently graduated from high school acknowledge that they clearly understood the community college instructor's expectations for students, but they did not take them seriously at first:

"In high school, I could just walk into class, sweet talk the teacher, and then I'd get my grade and whatever. And college is more, 'Okay, here's your syllabus, every day what we're gonna do is all listed on a certain date' — and no surprises, it's all written here on paper. And if you forget to look at your syllabus, you're like, there's my grade. And the grades here are not as easy to come by as grades in a public high school."

Students often report that even though instructors are typically clear about their policies, they are inconsistent in implementing certain policies, such as the number of classes students can miss, and policies vary for different instructors:

"They don't really care if you miss class 'cause that's your fault."

"Yeah, [attendance policy] depends on the professor."

"You can miss a class … I am. I already planned."

Whether or not an instructor stands firm on an attendance policy, students report that if they skip class, then they fall behind quickly. This frequently comes as an unpleasant surprise to new students who really did not understand the pace of college work and the price of poor attendance. The damage often is greatest when students miss classes early in the academic term:

"English [is hard right now] since I've skipped it a couple times. If you skip a class, you don't know what's going on the next day. Like a lot of stuff happens in one day."

"Well, I was doing good, and then I put too many hours in [at work]. And then my anatomy class, I barely even showed up to it because it's like an 8:00 in the morning class. And then I started noticing my teachers coming up to me, and they're like, 'You're failing your classes.'"

More often than not, students say they appreciate those instructors who are firm regarding their policies and follow up with students who disregard them:

"You can't miss more than two days [and] she doesn't want you being a minute late. She's a cool teacher … she set our rules the first day and let us know, 'You got two days to miss or you're going to be dropped, and they better be valid excuses.' That's the one class where everybody really shows up. But in my other class, people come and go, people come in an hour late; it can be the last 20 minutes of class, and people just walk in, and [the teacher] doesn't say anything — she doesn't talk to them after class."

"They're really big on [class attendance]. They will send you to your advisor if you miss too many classes. They give you the option of dropping the class and starting again, or they tell you, 'Look, you either need to be there or not.'"

Classes that Work and Those that Do Not

On *SENSE*, students report to what extent they are experiencing learning strategies that are critical for their success. Some of these activities occur in class; others occur outside of class as part of assigned work or because, as students describe in focus groups, their activities during class have prompted them to continue working with their classmates. They paint a picture of a class that does not engage them and contrast it with classes that bring their learning alive.

Classes that Do Not Work

"[The teacher is] a real nice lady, good teacher, but all that talking, it gets so boring after a while. And you know, it sucks, because I don't want to get tired, I want to listen, but I work late and it's not very lively."

"It's just so hard to stay awake in class and just sit there 'cause he just talks; he just reads the stuff that's on the overhead, and it's so hard to just sit there and pay attention and not fall asleep."

"She's going to read it pretty much verbatim off the slide. So it's like, 'Come on, tell us a side note or something that's not on the PowerPoint slide. I can read this at home.'"

"I swear, I don't know how she does it; I don't know how you can sit there and talk for an hour and fifteen minutes. She just talks the entire time we're in class, the entire time."

— Community college student

Classes that Work

"There's a lot of interactive activity with students and teachers in my speech class. I love speech class. The teacher may have you do an assignment on your own and then present it to the class, and the class gives feedback. The interaction is so important, especially with the teacher."

"We had to go up in front of the class twice, but the first one was a group. And according to the professor you do this so when you do it on your own you'll feel more comfortable."

"Like in a terminology class that I'm in now, we play Jeopardy during the weekday with some of the words that we need to know the definitions of and try to earn extra-credit points. So there's always some kind of activity to keep things rolling and interesting."

"All of my classes are learn labs, and I think that makes it a lot better because it's so interactive, you get to discuss things in a small group — it does help to increase participation in the class. You don't have to say it in front of the whole class; you say it in front of your little group. The teacher's so enthusiastic about the material, and it does make it more exciting and interesting to be there, learning from them."

"I enjoy the learn labs a lot. It takes you out of your shell because you have to interact with people and give your ideas and thoughts and show your work and be criticized."

Learning by Doing

Students frequently articulate the high value that they place on the kinds of learning that require them to perform real tasks. It is also enormously helpful if those tasks have clear relevance to work that they could find themselves doing in the future, but even just connecting the classroom to out-of-class activities is a major plus:

> *"The big thing for me is not just to learn about something, but to actually do it, and it's that hands-on approach that I love about this school. You learn a topic and then the instructor turns around and says, 'Okay, show me.'"*

> *"We have a lab in the classroom, and I'm in radiology so we kind of practice on each other, like our partner's the patient. Now I'm at the hospital three days a week, working just like a regular employee, going to surgery, and working beside the radiologist. We interact and have a lot of group activities."*

> *"I'm participating in the Cardinal Cravings Store; we get to run the store. We're split into five different groups, and we use our own marketing strategies. It's a very hands-on project."*

> *"Our assignments make us go and be a part of student activities, which I didn't do too much before. So now I'm going to all these campus events and going to the library. I'm all studious."*

Encouraging Student Effort

On *CCSSE*, only 52% of students say they *often* or *very often* are working harder than they thought they could to meet an instructor's expectations. Ten percent of students say they are *never* working harder than they thought they could to meet expectations. Even while students acknowledge that they might complain about a class that is challenging for them, many say their difficult classes are the ones they most appreciate. Students are quick to list the types of teachers and learning opportunities that keep them motivated:

> *"She had a reputation of just being really tough, and her classes were really tough, it was a lot of work, but it's five credits, it's what you signed up for when you went into*

it. But having that base of knowledge that I have after making it through her class, it's just indispensable."

"Sternness. Not too stern, but stern enough to know when you're slipping. Not so much where they're going to call your mom, but, at the same time, they let you know when you need to bring it up a bit. They want to see me in class; they want to see me do well."

"My anatomy professor, he was a very strict professor, and everyone always said he was hard and mean, but I'm used to that strictness. If he saw you doing your hardest, he would help you, he would bend over backward to help you more. Every time I see him, he tries to encourage me and gives me tips on how to learn something better."

"He makes me think hard, like so much about certain situations, about current events and stuff. I learned a lot. I mean, it keeps me thinking, you know?"

"[Teachers] will even go so far as to challenge you to do better on the next test. I got a 95 on one test, and he said, 'That's all? You can't get 100?'"

"Every teacher is always pushing me to do better, but they don't push me in a way that would push my buttons or upset me. They are always encouraging and, for me, that's the best way to go. If you can't encourage your students to do better, then you don't need to be a teacher."

> **"I always end up appreciating teachers that are hard on me. I mean, I hate it at the moment, but my favorite teachers are always the ass kickers."**
>
> — Community college student

Doing Work that Is Relevant

Asked how much time they spend preparing for class, on *SENSE,* the majority of full-time students (56%) report that they spend five or fewer hours per week. While students in focus groups acknowledge that they struggle to balance the demands of school and other commitments, they also report that they are far more likely to continue their work outside of class if they believe the work is valuable, relevant, and *required:*

"I'm [studying] 45 hours a week beyond classes. This was a big surprise to me. The only thing that upsets me is when it's busy work. I used to have a life other than school. I don't mind it being school right now, but I would love to have some control over the relevancy versus the busy work."

"I mean, I read what needs to be read; other than that I tend not to study 'cause they lecture over it in class — well, certainly my teachers do. They lecture over what they wanted you to read the night before, so reading seems pointless, often, once you go and you sit there and you're like, 'Why am I even here? You're telling me everything I read last night.'"

"I'm just so excited about my computer science class that … when I go home, the first thing that I do is my homework. It's all of the information that I'm taking in from it. I go through and read the book, even sections that … I'm not required to read, just because I want to learn more. It inspires you to look into something a bit deeper than what your class is requiring of you."

Seeing the Possibilities

At its best, college is often a time of discovery. In the community college, in particular, there are opportunities for faculty, advisors, and students themselves to open up previously unimagined opportunities, undiscovered interests and talents, and utterly unpredictable aspirations:

"I didn't know I can act, and I was on stage this last spring in the EL Theater, and I've produced music because of my music teachers' encouragement. Yeah, the instructors here are very positive."

"I kind of want to go to Europe now … Italy and France and all those places, so I can look at the artwork by, like, Donatello and Michelangelo, and these famous artists. There's more to art than I ever thought. It's not just painting. It's everything. I really like art history. We went to the art museum downtown, and then we went to the Menil [Collection] last Saturday. So it's different artwork. It's not just Roman and Greek. There's also artwork of today's generation. You can compare what art has become today over the years and the centuries. I like it a lot. Well, reading and looking at pictures is fun, too — but getting out is better."

"I came here from a family where no one ever had been to college. I thought I wanted to get a nursing assistant certificate, and then, you know, my first nursing instructor, she told me to dream bigger — that I could do more, be more. So now I'm gonna go to medical school."

Learning in Community

Having listened to students speaking at length about the importance of their relationships at the college, about the value of working in groups with their classmates, and about classes that help them connect with subject matter, it comes as no surprise to hear them describe positive experiences with organized learning communities on their campuses. While faculty and administrators tend to fret about bureaucratic and logistical complexities (how to make class schedules and room assignments work), students get to the heart of the matter:

> "I thought college was gonna be like this horrible, oh-my-gosh-I-can't-believe-I'm-doing-this experience, but I'm in the [first-year experience] learning community at my school, and like I said, it's a big help from that transfer from high school to college. And when I got to class I was like, 'Is this it? Is this what they've been telling us about?' It's not scary at all."

> "I'm currently taking Mexican-American history and English 101. I [like it] just because [of] the fact that you share the grade for both the classes, and it's not just focused on English. And they merge them both, so obviously your papers are gonna be on Mexican-American history, but you're still learning the essentials you need for an English 101 class. I think it's a good idea. Class size is really big, but if you merge two classes … it's gonna get like that. You still get your 10-minute break in between so you're not sitting down for three hours straight. We have two separate instructors — one for each respective class. You get both your history credit and your English credit. They consider it as one whole six-hour credit. Learning community classes I really recommend. Take 'em, they're fun. It's a good way to get credits."

> "All my English assignments are based from my engineering class, so it helps both of them out. It works out pretty well."

> "I like it a lot because classes are linked together. You're moving across the campus to go to your next class, and you work with a lot of the same people. It's easier to work with other people and find people to work with instead of transitioning from one class to the other."

Accelerating Progress

Students who have placed into developmental courses often express frustration that they must remain in the same developmental course for an entire semester, particularly when they believe they could move more quickly through the material. Even when students acknowledge that they probably do need to refresh their understanding of basic math and English, they often report that they catch on quickly once they start reviewing concepts and that they should have an opportunity to move ahead at their own pace. "They just move so slow — and I know I'm developmental, but I'm not slow." Those students in accelerated or "fast-track" courses, often augmented with online programs or with supplemental instruction, generally say they appreciate having that option and are progressing quickly to go on to the next level. For some students, however, the pace of accelerated courses presents challenges, and they often need — and usually receive — extra help:

"You better catch on real quick."

"You've got to work extra hard to catch up, and if you don't, you're probably gonna fail whatever she taught that day."

"The computer-aided math is simple. God, I wish they'd taught it like this in high school, and I wouldn't have had so many problems. I'm doing better in math now at 31 than at 14. I feel comfortable with it."

Do You Know How You Are Doing?

During the first three weeks of college, 93% of new students report on the *SENSE* survey that they have received grades or points on assignments or tests at least once. However, when asked if they have received *prompt feedback* from their instructors, 26% of new students say they never received prompt written or oral feedback from instructors on their performance. Whether they have received that type of feedback or not, many students in focus groups say they are not at all sure how they are doing in their classes:

"I feel like I'm just floating, man. I'm not doing any greater than I should, I don't think. Maybe so."

Students quickly learn that there is no consistency in the way instructors provide feedback. They have to figure out each instructor's method:

"Lots of teachers have their own way [of posting grades]. Some will take out their grade book and let you know 'this is your grade, and this is what you're missing.' Some post online and tell you to look it up. Some depend on you to keep track of your own grade."

Students make clear that the ways instructors communicate about their academic performance do not line up with how many students have been accustomed to learning about their progress and, as a result, the information often is not useful to them. No matter how instructors provide feedback, students too often struggle to figure out how they are doing in class, as the following conversation illustrates:

"I don't understand the grading that they do here. I'm just waiting. My teacher will tell me. I don't know my exact grade."

"It's not like a solid 'this is what you have.' It's more like 'look at all this and you figure it out.'"

"In my speech class, it's like you got a 1700 out of a 1900. I'm like, so um, I don't know what that is. It sounds pretty good, but I'm not sure."

"You ask them your grade, and they might tell you, but you might not understand it. They tell you, 'You need to do this work.' 'Okay, so what's my grade?' You just have to find out at the end of the semester, and you'll be surprised."

"I just want to know what it is. I understand that I'm fine. I just want to know what it is. A or B."

"Yeah, mine are [online], but I don't really know what they are; [I'm] waiting for that letter grade."

The Faculty Perspective

Students and faculty have widely differing perceptions about the extent to which instructors provide prompt feedback. On the Community College Faculty Survey of Student Engagement *(CCFSSE)*, 92% of faculty report that they provide prompt feedback to students *often* or *very often*. Yet on the student survey *(CCSSE)*, only 57% of students report frequently receiving prompt feedback. Many instructors are, however, aware that students struggle with understanding the information faculty give them:

"[Students] should know all the time how they're doing. I have students who ask me at mid-term, 'How did you get that grade?' That is a problem for them. I don't know how to solve that. You need to keep a list in your notebook of every essay grade and every quiz grade. It confounds me!"

"[Students need] an understanding of what the GPA is. They don't know how to calculate that, how important that is in relation to their status, as being on the verge of [academic] probation. That's what Freshman Seminar does. We designed a packet where they have to project their GPA, and once they access mid-term grades, then they can review their GPA with the one they predicted."

Getting Help

Within the first few weeks of their first term, many students say they have quickly fallen behind:

"All of a sudden I was behind a couple of assignments. And then the next day, behind more assignments. And then after that, it was just overwhelming."

"My math teacher, she'll do the problem on the board, and I can see what she's doing here, but she does it so fast. I kind of don't want to be like, 'Can you stop and show me how to do this?' because there's about 30 other people in the class, and I don't want to be the oddball in the class and look around and people are watching me try to get this problem, 'cause it's just not what I want to do."

Entering Students Report that During the First Three Weeks of Class, They:

25%	*Never* asked an instructor for help
83%	*Never* participated in a study group outside of class (required or student-initiated)
69%	*Never* participated in supplemental instruction
85%	*Never* used face-to-face tutoring
64%	*Never* used writing, math, or other skill labs

0% 20% 40% 60% 80% 100%

SOURCE: 2011 *SENSE* COHORT DATA.

Worried that they do not know what steps to take to catch up, some students simply stop attending class and/or stop doing the assigned work. Many are unlikely to seek help on their own. Even when they find themselves floundering early in the term, 25% of students report that they *never* asked for help from an instructor. Asked on the *SENSE* survey whether they have used the college's tutoring services or skill labs, the overwhelming majority of students report that they have not. In this instance, as previously noted, responses differ for different age groups, with younger students — those 18–24 years old — less likely than nontraditional-age students to ask their instructors for help or access the available academic support services.

> "I was the one who had questions, and people would look at me funny like, 'Well, like, don't you get it?' And I really didn't."
>
> — Community college student

Use of Tutoring and Skill Labs

Within the first three weeks of their first academic term, 85% of entering students have never used the college's tutoring services, and almost two-thirds of students say they have not sought assistance in the writing, math, or other skill labs. Many acknowledge that they have already fallen behind in their classes and need extra help, but they just cannot bring themselves to seek it out, as the following conversation among several students illustrates:

"I just don't want to tell him, you know, 'I don't know how to do this. I need help.'"

"Some of it could just be because of pride."

"Yeah, I think that's what it mostly is."

"You know, you just sit there and say, 'I don't need help, I can do this,' and then you get home and you're just confused, and you're like, man, I should've [gone to the tutoring center].'"

"A lot of professors, they emphasize to go there; it'll help, so you've just got to swallow your pride, bite the bullet, and go."

Some students take the first step to seek help but have a hard time following through. Once they do, however, they are generally pleased with the results:

"I kind of walked in and walked out twice. And then I finally convinced myself to go in. It was one-on-one with a former student. It actually helped me a lot. I didn't expect them to be that much on tutoring. But they actually were. Every other class somebody comes in about the tutoring and just reminds you that they're there."

"I have algebra for two days a week. Basically every time I have that class I go straight to [math lab] after class. There's a lot of people in there that, even if you don't need help, they're constantly asking you, 'Hey, you need help? You need help? If you need help, just let me know.' And they actually help you. There's a lot of math whizzes in there, and they actually dumb it down for you to understand."

The Value of Study Groups

On *SENSE*, more than 83% of students report that during the first three weeks of class, they have not yet participated in a study group, either one assigned by their instructor or one that students in their class have initiated on their own. Those who have participated in study groups say studying with their peers creates new supports and makes it easier to ask for and accept help:

"Your study group is basically gonna be your biggest help, in my opinion, because being in that study group, you're learning and, at the same time, you're learning with your peers, and that helps out a lot."

"[Study groups] help form bonds with other people, and we look at each other go, 'Okay, are you as lost as I am?' and it's very comforting when they go, 'Yes, it's like a foreign language to me.'"

"I met a couple people that I actually do study groups with in the evenings. We get together if somebody needs help with something; either they call me or they'll call one of the other people, and we exchange information and stuff. So there's always somebody I know I can depend on to help me if I don't understand."

Supplemental Instruction

Getting help becomes easier, students report, when there is an individual in their class who is there specifically to provide help on site:

"Well, thankfully [anatomy and physiology] has an SI, a student instructor — it's a student who previously took the class, aced it, and knows this professor, this class. And you get together once a week, twice a week sometimes, and you go over the material that's been discussed in class, and anybody can come to it. So I got to meet a lot of great people doing that, and we've formed our own study group on top of that one just to help us out a little bit more. But it has really saved me big time."

The Qualities of a Good Teacher

Above all, students are clear and consistent in talking about the characteristics and actions of the teachers whom they believe are the best. With considerable insight, they describe not just the pedagogical skills but also the *humanity* that makes great teachers great. *Are we listening?*

"The more learning techniques a teacher has under their belt, they'll be able to reach a larger crowd. It makes you more qualified and a better teacher."

"If he knows we're not getting it, he'll go all over [it] again; he'll do it just for you. We have like 30 minutes where we're supposed to do our homework, and he'll go by every single person and be like, 'Are you getting it?' If he sees you're stuck, he'll give you step-by-step [instructions] and tell you what you're doing wrong and all that. So he's really good."

"When class ends, they don't just take off; they make sure if anybody has any questions, if they need help with anything. They just really want to make sure that you're learning, and they're taking care of you."

"I had a lit teacher, probably two or three semesters ago, who was really, really great because all he wanted was for his students to succeed, and he would do anything that he possibly could to help you get things done. He made the class really interesting, and he was always interested in what was going on in your life."

"They're friends, they listen — they take the time to listen. Their doors are always open; you can go there, and you don't feel that they're with an attitude that they're better than you. They are there as your colleagues, and that makes all the big difference."

"Everyone that I have had has been passionate about what they do, has been helpful, has been willing to mentor if you need help."

Faculty members and others reading here about student involvement in tutoring, skill labs, and other experiences traditionally categorized as "support services" might wonder why they are included in a chapter that is largely focused on what goes on in community college classrooms. The reason is straightforward, based on a conviction that is consistently supported by data from students: If participation in these experiences is based on a referral model — if the experiences are not incorporated in syllabi as requirements for courses — the students who need them most will too often simply opt out. The same axiom applies to supports that more often are formally attached to classes; study groups and supplemental instruction provide clear benefits, according to students, but they need to be integrated into the educational experience.

Decades of research on effective practice in undergraduate education have reinforced the value of student engagement — the extent to which students are involved in purposeful educational activities. The in-class and out-of-class experiences that students describe as helpful to their learning and persistence — whether active learning in the classroom, participation in tutoring or supplemental instruction, working in study groups, or receiving frequent feedback on their performance — all are consistent with that research. And all serve to intensify students' purposeful involvement — with one another, with faculty and support staff, and with the subject matter they study.

Jeffrey's Story

Jeffrey was full of plans and potential when he graduated from an arts and technology magnet school, but he is the first to admit he was not the best high school student. "I kind of played around. I had the potential to get the full scholarships and whatnot, graduate magna cum laude, but I chose to do the extracurriculars," says the former senior class president. Good at math and design, he envisioned a career in architecture. But when it became clear that he did not have the GPA to qualify for a university scholarship, he headed to a community college. "My high school counselor made community college seem so bad. But [once I was there] I'm like, 'this is a nice little place.'"

QUICKLY OVERWHELMED: In his first term, Jeffrey enrolled as a full-time student. It was too much for him. "I think it's easier for someone to come in and stay if they take their time, build up a habit for coming to school, get a study habit, and then start upgrading their classes and how they want to do their workload," he reflects. Jeffrey quickly returned to his high school patterns and put his energy into his social life.

CHALLENGES: Math had once been Jeffrey's favorite subject, but, to his surprise, he tested poorly on the college placement test and found himself bored and frustrated in a developmental math class. "My professor, she even told me, 'You're not supposed to be in here. You were taking calculus in high school.'"

He needed help in his American government class. Well aware that he could go to the tutoring center, Jeffrey was reluctant to try it. He preferred to get help at home, where he "wasn't embarrassed." "My brother took [the class]," Jeffrey explains. "He passed it. So when I needed a little help, I went to him."

Struggling with poor study habits and distracted by his social life, Jeffrey dropped out after the first semester.

FINDING WHAT WORKS: Jeffrey went to work at a grocery story and discovered he had a talent for retail work. He quickly progressed to a management track. The job is giving him a chance to grow gradually in an environment where he can see direct results. "I still study every day," Jeffrey says. "I have reports I have to pull everyday, that I look at, check out numbers, and get an understanding, so when I go into these meetings, I'm knowledgeable."

NEXT STEPS: Encouraged by his supervisor to continue his education, Jeffrey soon will complete his company's school of retail management and earn a promotion to department manager. Then he plans to re-enroll in community college as a business major. "Architecture was something I really wanted to do," says Jeffrey. "But what I love [now] is the retail business. So it'd be better for me to get a business degree. That way I can have a concept of everything that's going on at work."

As he prepares to return to school, Jeffrey is putting into place the crucial support he needs to stay focused. "Last time I was around people who were all about, 'Let's go to the student center,' or 'Let's go shoot pool,' or 'Let's go hang out.' Now I'm setting a crowd around me that really makes sure that my focus is in school. It's basically my boss and a few friends. They're all about, 'You need to get back into school, we got your back.' They're showing me there is a good thing about going back to school because it pays off in the end."

Meredith's Story

Meredith enjoys working with children, and most of the jobs she held while going to college reflect that. "I've always wanted to be a teacher," she says. The 23-year-old attended college off-and-on the last six years, but she says her attitude, finances, and lack of commitment temporarily derailed her: "Last summer I had an enlightenment. I thought, 'You've been wasting time and money, and if you want to be a teacher, you need a degree … so quit messing around.'" Meredith now is within reach of earning an associate degree in teaching.

GETTING STARTED: Although Meredith graduated from high school with a 3.8 GPA and average SAT scores, she lacked confidence when she enrolled at a university. She left the university after a year and a half and then enrolled at a local community college.

TAKING A BREAK: After one semester, Meredith decided to take a break from school. She joined a nonprofit organization dedicated to ending violent conflict in Uganda. "I was drawn to them because it seemed cool, youthful, and innovative, and I have always been interested in helping children," she says.

RETURNING AGAIN TO COLLEGE: Now, while working full-time, Meredith is once again enrolled in the community college. Her overall experience is positive: "Part of what I like about the community college is that class size is much smaller and people know your name."

CHALLENGES: Unafraid to ask for help, Meredith found it was not always forthcoming. "One teacher was real defensive and said, 'If you read the book, you'll get it.' I was reading the book and I didn't get it," she says. Meredith dropped an online literature class. "I really need a teacher present — I ask a lot of questions. I tend not to manage my time well, and so I procrastinated," she explains. Another concern was the disconnect between her developmental and college-level math classes. "The remedial class was almost too simple. I feel like it didn't really prepare me. I was really awful in the next step."

FINDING WHAT WORKS: Meredith says one of the reasons she stayed with college this time is "because of teachers who tried to make me feel special. For the past two years, I've had really great teachers. [And] it's clear in my own mind that I'm not stupid."

Describing a philosophy class she liked, Meredith says, "It was difficult … but the teacher was passionate about philosophy and let us form our own opinions and debate them. It was active, not boring." She received an A in the class.

Although she dreaded college algebra, Meredith says she never had a better teacher. "There is some disconnect with me understanding math, and he bridged that gap. Honestly, no teacher had ever explained it like that before. I worked really hard, and he worked really hard with me."

Also engaging for Meredith was a repeat of the U.S. government course in which she previously made a D. This time the class featured more active learning. "If I have just a lecture, I get bored," Meredith says. One of her favorite assignments was writing her own version of the Declaration of Independence. "You had to really think of all the causes and effects … I loved it because it enabled me to think creatively and work outside the box, versus just memorizing."

NEXT STEPS: After she earns a bachelor's degree, Meredith hopes to teach at an inner city school. "I want to teach students who don't necessarily have the tools they need to succeed."

Jeremy's Story

For Jeremy, the transition from high school to college held some unusual challenges. But focus and persistence helped him overcome the obstacles in his path. He will soon earn his second associate degree and already has half his credits toward a bachelor's degree in biomedicine.

As a child, Jeremy struggled with juvenile rheumatoid arthritis. When he was in the 4th grade, the disease reached its peak, and his parents began home schooling him. They continued home schooling through high school. "Home schooling helped," says Jeremy. "I was able to stay on track and, at the same time, to rest when I needed to."

After graduating from high school, Jeremy enrolled in the community college near his home. "I really wanted to start college and better myself but felt not quite ready for university level. I thought that community college was a better place to prepare," he says.

GETTING STARTED: Because of his health problems, Jeremy was directed to the college's Center for Students with Disabilities. "With arthritis, you have good days and then you get hit pretty hard. It was reassuring to know I had extra help," he says. "There was an awesome counselor there who is still helping me out today." When he initially struggled in his developmental math class, Jeremy was directed to the college's tutoring services. "It was really helpful — I've gotten A's in all my math classes here."

FINDING WHAT WORKS: Encouraged by a friend, Jeremy became involved in a student leadership program at the college and in Student Technology Services (STS), a work-based program. "Students are placed in a department related to their major to get hands-on experience," says Jeremy, who began at a help desk and moved up to become one of four student managers.

Jeremy believes he has benefited from the unusual relationship among all the high schools in his community, the community college, and the local university. The partnership helps prepare high school students for college and allows students to enroll simultaneously at the community college and university. As a result, there are no issues with articulation and transferring.

In his last semester of high school, Jeremy took a dual-enrollment class in English. When he started college, he was undecided about a major. "I knew I could get the basic courses and didn't need to decide right away," he says. Jeremy earned an associate degree, enrolled at the university, and now takes classes at both institutions. He works part-time at the community college while seeking a second associate degree in chemistry.

"Through my experiences I've learned more about time management," he says. Jeremy credits the high school/college/university relationship with giving students a chance to progress more rapidly. "All these doors opening up give students a chance to make something of themselves at a really young age," he says. "It gave me some hope."

NEXT STEPS: Pursuing degrees in science, Jeremy is considering becoming a physician. "I grew up with medical problems, but I learned a lot about how to take care of myself and others. I know I can put that to good use," he says. For now, though, he is struggling a little. "I'm taking so many classes, and I have to work," he says. "I've lost a little focus. I'm a little tired."

ADVICE TO THE COLLEGE: Jeremy encourages those who work at community colleges to keep their focus on the ultimate goal of community colleges — student success. Faculty, he says, "should want more for your students."

CHAPTER 7

Disengaging: Now You See Me, Now You Don't

> "It's a goal that I've had set my whole life … to go to college and get a degree — and I'm gonna finish whether I need to or not, that's what I'm gonna do. And whether it's a degree that I'll use, I mean I'll prefer to use it in the future, but even if I change my mind, I'm gonna leave this college with a degree."
>
> — Community college student

Despite what they say they about their college goals when they first enroll, almost half of community college students leave college before the beginning of their second year.[1] And by six years after entry, only 45% of those who stated their goal was an associate degree or higher have earned an associate degree or bachelor's degree, transferred to a four-year institution, or are still actively enrolled at a community college.[2] At the beginning of their first college year, students typically describe enthusiastically why they have come to college and express commitment to achieving their goals. Following students in focus groups throughout their first year, we hear how things change as the year progresses.

James

A recent high school graduate, James enrolls as a full-time student and is majoring in music. While in high school, he earned credit for two college courses — one in college algebra and another in English. He has a scholarship to attend college.

August, before classes begin:

> *"I've always wanted to go to college. Nobody in my family has ever gone to college, so I'm the first, and I do it for my little brother, my little sister, and all my nieces and nephews. [I want] to show the younger generation of my family you don't have to drop out; you don't have to, you know, accidentally have a child in high school. It doesn't have to be like that. You can go to college, you can do what you want to do, so long as you got your head on straight."*

"I'm hoping for [a] challenge. I like to push myself mentally. I like to listen in and learn new things, and I know that's what college is all about. They teach me stuff high school won't. And I'm all about learning new things. I love education."

James has just taken the placement test and tested into developmental reading:

"... Not 'cause it was hard, but because I kind of just rushed through it. I didn't really read it very well. It was really my fault. And I was supposed to come back two days later, on a Thursday. And I was gonna re-do it. I only missed it by like two, three points ... . Reading's my strongest subject, but I don't know. Anyways, I was gonna come back, and I was an hour late, so I have to put up with that class. I'm gonna take this test in September to get out of it. I mean, reading is not hard, it's just, I wasn't concentrating. It was my fault."

James is worried about potential challenges in college:

"Between school and work and what I have to do at home and [music] performances, it'll be hard."

"If you have a teacher out there that's interactive and he has a lot of energy, brings out a lot of energy, and he makes learning fun, and then if he's funny or whatever, if he gives something out, that kind of stuff helps you stay awake, helps you stay focused. That's another thing I'm worried about. Classes being boring. I don't do well with boring."

September, three weeks into the term:

"I have to admit I was nervous. Like any incoming freshman. But ... you just gotta see it as ... just another day at school. You just adapt to it, I mean I did. It's easy. It's just a lot of homework. I don't like homework."

"I just got my books. I just got one, the last one that I needed, maybe last Friday, and they just had ... got some in. See, every time I go, that particular book was never in stock, so I would just kind of catch them at bad times. It was hard, but now you've got the book, you don't got to borrow nobody's book to do the homework. Luckily, I had a friend in that class ... but if you've got your own stuff, it's easier."

"Her class is real dim lighted, and she talks with a softer voice, and then ... she starts talking to us about the assignment or whatever and ... she's just talking and I'm trying to listen, and then I notice that I get tired really fast. And, you know, it sucks because I don't want to get tired, I want to listen, but I work late and it's not very lively."

"I like to associate myself around people who are attentive and who take notes and who ask questions and stuff like that. Even though I don't do that all the time ... you learn off other people. [Someone else might] ask a question that I wanted to know, but

I didn't want to ask because of being nervous or people thinking I'm dumb for not knowing the question. Stuff like that will really help somebody else out. It's really a lot on the students, too, it's not just on teachers. It's up to us to make the best of it."

James acknowledges that sometimes he skips class, that college is harder than he thought it would be, and that he is trying to balance school and work:

"I just didn't want to go to school. I was tired, and I didn't feel like going. I didn't feel like driving 20 minutes just to go to school."

"Yeah, you're going to college, man, you should take the initiative. Me, I'm so fresh out of high school, and I'm used to all my teachers … not so much helping me, but in high school they basically babysit you, especially me. I was a senior in high school … basically all I did was just show up to class, and I was so cool with my teachers, they just passed me."

"I'm at school and if I'm not at school, I'm at work. I don't really see anybody outside of class."

November, after midterms:

"Well, I like my classes, not because they're easy, that's not it, but because of the people I'm around. I'm around a bunch of people who are willing to learn and around people who want to learn and to me that's what's most important. It's easier to learn when you want to learn. You can't learn if you don't want to. Like they say, you can take the horse to water, but you can't make him drink. And my teachers, they're willing to work with you so long as you're willing to work with them."

"It's college, you have to do a lot of homework. That's just how it is. High school, when you're a senior in high school, everything's spoon-fed to you. College, it's all on you. In high school, teachers help you, put it down for you, they help you with your grades or whatever. College, it's just all on you. You want it, you get it."

"Midterms were kinda, you know, studying for that. I have a study problem too because I don't have time and because — I gotta be honest — I hate studying. I just don't enjoy it at all. It's boring. You're just there. But you need to do it in order to do well in your classes. I know that I'm probably, say, a C — but I'm probably doing a little bit better than that. It is what it is."

"I've missed a few days. Missing definitely sucks because of all the stuff you need to go and ask for what was talked about, maybe consult with some of your peers, some of your classmates, see what was going on. 'Cause the teacher, a lot of teachers, all they'll tell you is, 'Look on Blackboard.' It's like, yeah, Blackboard tells me the subject, but I want to know what we covered. It's just stuff like that, and then the homework — and God forbid there was a quiz that day you missed, and some teachers aren't as lenient about make-up tests and stuff like that. It sucks."

James has reconsidered his college plans:

"I like the people. I like the environment. I like the classes. It's just, driving over and back 20 minutes a day to and from home. It took me 20 minutes to get here. It takes me 20, almost 30, minutes to get home. So that's one of the things. And then the classes aren't exactly all that hard; it's just that I don't really want to do it. It's nothing about the school. The school's fine. The school's the school. It's me. Right now it just feels like I need to go do something else."

"School's all right. I like it, but it's not for everybody, and I guess I'm just one of those people that it's not for. Maybe sometime later on in life I'll pick it back up again. It is what it is. As far as next term, what I plan on doing is I'm joining the military. I'm joining the Air Force — so yeah, I'm gonna go do that."

James drops out of college in late November.

March, James is no longer attending the college:

"I was a major in music, and my goal was to just get an associate [degree] and move on to a bigger and better school — but that was my long-term goal, I know that. My goal hasn't changed. It just got delayed; you know, it happens."

"I just stopped coming due to personal things at the house, and I just had to stop coming, and I regret it, I do; like I say, things happen, they all happen for a reason. It's okay, I'll be back."

"[When I left], I talked to one teacher on Facebook. Actually, it was a teacher who told me to get a Facebook, and I just let her know I wasn't coming back. I talked to my music instructor, too. I called him on his cell phone. I more or less explained my situation. I really didn't go into detail. But I told him, 'Look, things happen, I'm not going to be able to come back, for at least not until the fall, because this and that.' But I explained to him that I wasn't coming back, it is what it is. Yeah, I mean he was like, 'Well, I really wish you wouldn't. I really wish you would reconsider.' Doing the good teacher thing, because he really is a good teacher; but he goes, 'You have to do what you have to do, so take care of it. We'll see you next time.' All right, cool."

James has not yet joined the military and says he wants to return to school:

"Ultimately, at the end of the day, I want to come back to school. And it's something I am very adamant about and something that I strive for a lot because I want to better myself by furthering my education. A high school diploma is not enough anymore … and I understand and realize that, so now I really need to do something with myself."

"I didn't think college was for me because it's really on me, I'm not gonna blame nobody. I'm a grownup now, so I can say it: I'm a big-time procrastinator. When it comes to schoolwork, I tend to be a little more laid back than I should. Like I said

earlier, it's more on you in college. So with that being said, and then my study habits, I never properly studied a day in my life. So it was like, maybe it's not all cracked up to what it was or what they made it seem. I was just being dumb, misguided, and arrogant, really. I don't think the same way anymore."

Ernie

Ernie is an older student. He has been working for a number of years and now is starting college.

August, before classes begin:

"I'm actually going in for a certificate and then maybe to an associate's [degree], if I can handle it."

September, three weeks into the term:

Ernie is in college because he thinks it will change his life:

"My mom didn't graduate, my dad didn't graduate, you know, my sister, she's going to college right now. And one of my sisters is not, so I just want to be able to do something different. I don't want to complete the cycle, I want to change things just a tad. None of my family really cares too much about their lives so ... that motivates me. So when I start drifting off ... I think about, I have to do this, to better [myself]."

November, after midterms:

Ernie is not connecting with people on his college campus:

"There's a lot of young kids, you know, so I don't even know anybody. I say 'hi,' but I'm just in class, and then once I'm done, I leave. I'm just the type of person I'm just going to go in and if I do see or meet somebody I won't deny it, I'll embrace it, but [I'm] not necessarily planning to look for anybody particularly."

Ernie does not think his classes are too hard, but he is not sure how he is doing:

"Some of the teachers will tell you, 'Hey, this is what [you're] missing. This is what you need." I feel like I'm just floating, man. I'm not doing any greater than I should, I don't think. Maybe so, but ... ."

... and he is not seeking help:

"They do talk about the help that you can get, so there's help out there — but, for me, I haven't gotten to that point yet, maybe I won't ever; hopefully I won't."

March, Ernie is no longer attending the college:

Ernie fails all his courses in the first term and is no longer attending the college:

> "The goal was to complete my certificate and start working in the field. It's kind of been on hold right now, but I can still achieve the goal I set."

When asked if he knows what percentage of students drop out of community college before their second year, Ernie guesses that it is nearly half:

> "Just going through it. Knowing how easy it is to fall and slide back. I guess that's the only way I would guess that high is 'cause I was in it and now I'm just kind of pushed back, so I fall into that percentage."

Ernie thinks about what happened that caused him to stop attending classes, to make failing grades, and, ultimately, to drop out:

> "As time passed, you kind of got used to a certain thing. You started to know that a teacher will kind of let you be late, let you slide on [being] absent. You just start getting detached from what was your goal. Some teachers were less tolerant than others. Some would take roll, some would not. For me, if I can find a way out, I get out of it."

> "It was probably midway, I just kind of fell back and just was like, 'I can wait just a little while.' I got overwhelmed sometimes with a full load. Being out of school so long. It was just kind of real frustrating."

> "I was stunned because it was just so fast-paced. To the point of where I missed a certain class once or twice, I was so far back where I was just like, 'Well, I'll just make it up on the test,' and then the test would pass. And you lost it. I don't know."

> "[Knowing] my grades was kind of a guess. Some teachers were real solid about it. They would keep you up to date on what you needed, what you didn't have in, your grades on those. And some, there was no communication at all. If I wasn't doing a certain thing, [then] I wouldn't know it or if I needed to do it, [then] I didn't know it. There was just no communication at all."

> "Well, I got the letters that were saying that I had been dropped for missing a certain amount of classes. I'm not sure the number, but it's not too high a number. And that was just it. It wasn't a warning saying, 'If you miss another day, I'm gonna drop you.' It was just kind of like a letter in the mail and that's it."

> "I just didn't take it serious. I felt that if I can get away with it, I'd try. Eventually, it just blew up in my face."

Ernie never asks for help when he falls behind in his classes:

"No, I guess it's easier said than done. Never bit the bullet. Maybe I was just worried about my image. I don't know. I just never did. I needed it. But never wanted to go that extra [step] and ask for help. I kind of just let it slip away."

What Is a College To Do?

Students offer different reasons for leaving college — reasons that are repeated by many. "I got a good job." "I got sick." "My kids were sick, and I couldn't keep up." "I was working too many hours; it was too much." "I guess college isn't for me." "I got so behind in my work that I couldn't catch up, so I didn't go back." But regardless of their stated reason, the result is the same. They begin with goals, motivation, and enthusiasm, but then they leave.

After dropping out, when asked about their future plans, students almost always give the same answers: "I want to come back." "I need an education." They talk about what will make it possible for them to return or what will have to change when they re-enroll. "Once the kids start school … ." "I'll have to go part-time — I can't manage school with working so much and taking care of my family." "I have to earn more money so I don't have to work so much when I go to school." "I have to grow up a little first." "I have to get over this feeling that I don't belong in college."

> "I believe everybody has their own motivation and demons, so it's just like you gotta weigh 'em out. What's the most important [thing] to you in your life? Is it schooling or is it working? So you gotta just kind of find it in yourself to push you through it. Because it's gonna be hard. Whether you look at it as if you get it easy or not, it's still gonna be tough because it's just something that you have to do."
>
> — Community college student

They all say, and clearly believe, that they will return to college and eventually earn the certificate or degree they want. But data show that many of them never return. Six years after initial entry, 46% of community college students have disappeared, without a certificate, degree, or transfer.[3]

It might be tempting to conclude that students know best about when it is the right time for them to go to college. Some might say that certain students simply are not ready the first time they enroll, that they have too much on their plates to succeed, that it is a good thing for them to step away and try again later. *And, after all, how much more can the college really do to overcome the obstacles students face in their personal lives or make up for their lack of self-discipline?* Students say and clearly believe that "it's all on me." When we ask students who have dropped out what more the college could have done to make it possible for them to stay, they are hard-pressed to think of anything. Nearly always, they see dropping out as a personal failure.

It might be comforting to conclude that there is nothing more colleges can or should do to help students succeed *if all things were equal*. However, all things are rarely equal — and that is where the discomfort kicks in. Among all students, some groups are far more likely to drop out and also less likely, once gone, to return: men, particularly men of color; students of color more generally, especially blacks, Latinos, and Native Americans; low-income men and women; and students who must complete multiple semesters of developmental education before they qualify for college-level courses.[4] For the sake of these students and their families, their communities, and the country, colleges cannot afford to answer these data with the sad and silent shrug.

Happily, not all students who face challenges drop out of college:

> *"Last quarter, I left because I was having some medical issues, and everybody was like, 'Where'd Lisa go? Where is she?' And they pretty much kind of tried to hunt me down. And I came back, and I said, 'I'm okay, I'm still alive, I'm here.' And they were like, 'Good, don't ever do that to us again.'"*

> *"Well, for me, having the teacher call, it was really a motivation. It made me feel like they do care about you and your well-being. That's really the only thing. They enforce pretty well what you need to do to stay focused, and the peer tutors and everybody there helping you. They're pretty dead on except for maybe the one-on-one. Maybe get on an individual level with each student."*

The Faculty Perspective

An interesting thing happens when faculty views on the reasons students drop out of community colleges are compared to students' reports on the same question. Typically, faculty members are much more likely to give weight to the external factors that they know impinge on students' college commitments.

Of course, students do often talk about the challenges of setting priorities, managing time, and learning to "do college" more effectively. And they typically take full responsibility for their failures. But listening carefully to their stories of leaving college, one can hear the themes: the need for personal connection, the essential value of clear expectations that are consistently enforced, the imperative of early intervention, the "stickiness" of engaged learning and peer relationships, the attraction of college work connected to a life's work, and the benefit of integrated *(mandatory)* academic support. These are themes on which colleges can act.

Community college students disengage at alarming rates. Clearly, they disappear for myriad reasons; just as clearly, there are some reasons that institutions will never be able to control. But students tell us through their stories — intentionally or not — that when colleges assume collective responsibility for student success, there is much that can yet be done.

How might students' educational prospects — and their lives — be affected if faculty and staff collaboratively design and diligently implement clear and coherent evidence-based educational pathways for every student? What if faculties committed to engaged learning as the hallmark of their colleges? What would be possible if every college faculty and staff member took responsibility for making personal connections with students — as part of every effort designed to help more students stay in college?

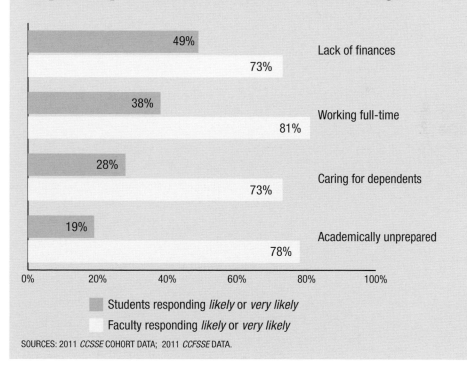

How Likely Is It that One or More of the Following Reasons Would Cause You [Students] To Withdraw from Class or from this College?

- Lack of finances: Students 49%, Faculty 73%
- Working full-time: Students 38%, Faculty 81%
- Caring for dependents: Students 28%, Faculty 73%
- Academically unprepared: Students 19%, Faculty 78%

Students responding *likely* or *very likely*
Faculty responding *likely* or *very likely*

SOURCES: 2011 *CCSSE* COHORT DATA; 2011 *CCFSSE* DATA.

CHAPTER 8

Community Colleges: Doing What Works for Students

In growing numbers, leaders at community colleges are collaborating within their own institutions, partnering with high school and university leaders, and reaching out to their communities to create pathways for students into and through higher education.

The following pages feature highlights of college initiatives that exemplify a range of approaches designed to help students prepare for college and to support new students in making a successful transition. These college initiatives reflect goals that include promoting a college-going culture in the community, ensuring that high school students are college-ready before they graduate, helping students transition to the community college, and supporting new students from their first contact with the college through the critical first year.

The variety of approaches reflects the reality that there is no single solution for strengthening student success. As respected researcher Patrick Terenzini cautions, "Do not zero in on finding the silver bullet. There aren't any."[1] Instead, colleges are implementing an array of strategies that tackle different challenges students face. Effectiveness is a product not of singular approaches but of an intentionally designed combination of strategies, as colleges work to weave them into a coherent educational experience.

Each of the following examples begins with a specific area of focus and then describes additional interventions that the college has put in place to enhance and expand efforts to effectively meet the needs of its diverse students.

Building College Knowledge
Houston Community College (TX)

Houston Community College (HCC) is one of the largest higher education institutions in the country, serving a diverse population of more than 60,000 credit students on multiple campuses.

Building Skills for Academic Success

Beginning in 2007, HCC phased in the requirement that all new and transferring students who have earned fewer than 12 semester hours take a student success course at the college. HCC offers different versions of the course for students with undeclared majors and students interested in engineering, health care, teaching, and the workforce. The course is designed to prepare students for the demands of college and for success in the workplace. One or more versions of the course now are offered at all 23 HCC locations.

Guided Studies 1270, the course designed for students who have not yet declared a major, emphasizes priority setting, time management, effective listening, information retention, note taking, critical thinking, problem solving, and test-taking skills. In addition to attending classes, students attend two mandatory career conferences that showcase HCC programs and help students with planning and setting educational objectives, career assessment, decision-making, and using library databases for research. Students are required to declare a major and file a degree plan by the end of the semester, steps that college leaders believe will build their momentum and enhance their subsequent success. The college currently is converting this course to a credit-bearing, transferable course that will address the current course objectives and incorporate additional learning strategies.

Showing Results

Even as the college's enrollment continues to grow, the persistence rates for students completing this course are improving and far exceed the persistence rates of students who initially enrolled in the college before the requirement to take a student success course went into effect. Fall-to-spring persistence of 2009 cohorts showed improvement for all ethnic groups, except for Asian students, whose 78% persistence rate has remained constant. Black students have made the greatest gains, with a persistence rate increase from 69% to 75%.

HCC's student success course became the foundation of the college's involvement in Achieving the Dream (AtD), a national initiative focused on improving community college student success. Although HCC had traditionally used data to inform decision-making at the institutional level, college leaders say that involvement in AtD pushed them to be more rigorous, examine data in multiple ways, and quickly take appropriate action.

Early Intervention

HCC continues to look at current practices and ask the question, "Do students need an additional hurdle to jump?" College personnel are careful to consider the student as an individual and to implement programs that provide clear academic guidance, ensure early intervention, and respect students' busy schedules. A move to intrusive advising is yielding good results; those results have turned around an old perception held by many at the college that the approach would turn students off, leading them to choose not to attend the college. After adding intrusive advising, the college is finding that its *CCSSE* results continually show a strength in the areas of student participation in career counseling and helping students to cope with their multiple responsibilities.

Learning Communities for Developmental Students

The college also has expanded its learning communities in developmental math. An external evaluation of HCC's learning communities by MDRC showed that students enrolled in the learning communities — particularly Hispanic students — were more likely to pass developmental math than students enrolled in stand-alone courses. Sixty-four percent of Hispanic students enrolled in the learning communities completed the course with a grade of C or better compared with 48% in stand-alone developmental math courses. In addition, learning community students enrolled in the next math class in the sequence at higher rates. The greatest impacts of the learning communities occurred for students who entered college with the lowest math placement scores.

Learning in Community
Kingsborough Community College (NY)

A learning community experiment at Kingsborough Community College that started with a small pilot now enrolls 45% of all first-time students. The college's goal is to enroll 80% of first-time students in learning communities within five years.

Kingsborough Community College is part of The City University of New York and is Brooklyn's only community college. Located in a seaside, urban setting, Kingsborough serves more than 18,500 credit students. The college has a diverse student population coming from 142 countries. Forty-one percent of Kingsborough's students are from families that earn less than $20,000 in annual household income, 63% work full-time, and more than 70% of students receive financial aid.

Opening Doors — Embracing an Experiment

In 2003, Kingsborough was one of six community colleges selected to participate in the MDRC *Opening Doors* project, focused on learning communities. Though the concept of learning communities was not new, the idea of employing learning communities as part of a broader effort to increase persistence and completion among community college students was unique in 2003.

As part of the initiative, Kingsborough launched multiple learning communities for incoming freshmen. Groups of 25 or fewer students registered into three classes during their first semester: English (either college-level or developmental, based on proficiency); a standard college credit offering, such as sociology or health; and a student success course taught by a counselor. Academic counseling was available within the learning community, and students received textbook vouchers to offset costs.

The students participating in the initial *Opening Doors* learning communities were randomly selected from among 1,500 freshmen. They reflected the composition of the college community — most were 17–20 years of age, representing multiple racial and ethnic groups. The freshmen who were not selected to participate in the learning communities composed a control group so college leaders could compare success rates.

Faculty members teaching in each learning community were asked to work collaboratively on curriculum, coordinate assignments among the three courses included in the learning community, and work together in evaluating student progress.

From the beginning, college leaders determined that the courses would be rigorous and that faculty needed to build a strong understanding of how to effectively integrate work for students.

Showing Progress — Promising Results

The initial MDRC evaluation showed that students participating in *Opening Doors* at Kingsborough had a more integrated college experience and moved more quickly through the developmental English requirements. However, questions remained about whether students continued to be successful after they completed their first courses and the structure of the learning community was no longer present.

In the first two semesters of their enrollment at Kingsborough, students' fall-to-spring persistence rates in the *Opening Doors* program were a little more than two percentage points higher than the control group (77.4% vs. 75% the first year; 61.3% vs. 59.2% the second year). However, after three semesters, the program group was five percentage points ahead of the control group (52.9% vs. 47.8%). This led college leaders to conclude that persistence was more of a long-term result — although delayed, the final outcome for most students in learning communities has been positive.

Collaboration and Commitment

With outcomes that continue to be encouraging, the college community is extremely committed to learning communities. College leaders say *Opening Doors* at Kingsborough is not built on one person, but it is part of the infrastructure of the college — it is now the way they do business. Faculty and staff attend weekly meetings to discuss curriculum, trade ideas, and collaborate on projects. This time with colleagues allows for more cooperation between faculty and student services staff, and that has proven beneficial for all. Everyone who works on the front lines with new students is at the table. They listen to and learn from one another and continually bring definition to what it means to be student-centered. In addition, Kingsborough faculty and staff say the *Opening Doors* project definitely has influenced a cultural shift toward identifying and implementing evidence-based practices at the college.

Next Steps

Today, Kingsborough's learning communities are nationally recognized. In 2006, the Ford Foundation awarded Kingsborough a $100,000 grant to help replicate the program in colleges across the country. College staff members present the Kingsborough story at other community colleges and at conferences, helping those who seek to improve student success through the implementation of learning communities.

Committed to Communities
Skagit Valley College (WA)

Skagit Valley College was founded in 1926 and serves three rural counties in coastal northwest Washington state. Approximately 6,000 students attend classes at two campuses and two centers. The college is nationally recognized for its learning communities, which were implemented in 1986 in an effort to improve student learning.

Integrating Course Content

The *Learning Communities Program* intentionally combines two different courses, such as math and reading, to help students discover connections between areas of study and to foster deeper, more meaningful learning relationships between students and faculty. Two, and sometimes three, teaching faculty members work together to create integrated assignments and classroom activities that reinforce each subject and help students understand how the concepts and skills of the two subject areas are connected.

Creating Community for Developmental Students

The learning communities originally included developmental classes, but these were largely abandoned as the small college focused its efforts on learning communities comprising college-level classes so that students could meet the college's new transfer degree requirement of completing three learning communities. However, promising data about the level of engagement of students in learning communities from *CCSSE* led the college to bring back developmental learning communities. In 2005–06, the college changed policy to allow developmental learning communities to count toward degree requirements and ramped up the effort to put them into practice. *CCSSE* data showed that students in learning communities are more engaged, and college leaders wanted their most at-risk students to have that opportunity.

Integrating Support into the Developmental Learning Communities

In 2007, the college added a counseling component to the *Developmental Learning Communities*, which now serve about 120 students per year. The program pairs two courses and two teaching faculty and incorporates a counselor into the community to teach college success skills. The counselor helps students understand the importance of study skills and how to find a variety of resources. Both student outcomes and student feedback are showing that the college success component makes a real difference to them. Students in counselor-enhanced learning communities have a slightly higher GPA, as well as increased persistence and completion in the course. Interestingly, even students who know they might fail the course remain until the end of the term. Students explain that they have made connections with teachers, counselors, and other students. Faculty say that is what impresses them most — students are making the commitment to come to class even though they know they are going to have to retake the course. Says one college leader, "I think it's the connections they make with each other. It's all about relationships."

Now that learning communities are once again part of the fabric of developmental studies at the college, leaders believe that developmental students especially are benefiting from learning communities. The communities that form in the classes provide ongoing support for the students. If a student does not show up for a few days, then someone will call. If a car breaks down, then someone will pick up the student. The students are forming their own study groups. Faculty who teach in both stand-alone classes and learning communities observe anecdotally that this level of peer support does not happen to the same degree in a stand-alone class.

Collaboration

The *Counselor-Enhanced Developmental Learning Communities* started with a strong commitment from the college that has continued. Faculty members create the courses and present proposals that include learning outcomes and integrative assignments. Teachers and counselors make the time to work together. Faculty members teaching in the learning communities are enthusiastic about their work and report that the work they do within learning communities is "the best professional development we get — learning from each other." College leaders say they usually get more proposals than they can accommodate in the schedule.

Teaching faculty report that having a counselor in the classroom "really enhanced the connections made in the classroom and improved the interaction and dynamic for discussions and provided a different voice — a richness to skills development."

Showing Progress

In fall 2008, Skagit compared student performance in the *Counselor-Enhanced Developmental Learning Communities* to performance in corresponding stand-alone courses. In the learning communities, 74% of students passed the courses with a C or better, compared to 68% in stand-alone classes. In addition, persistence rates from fall to winter quarters were 91% for the learning communities, compared to 85% for stand-alone classes. The college's evaluation of results consistently includes analysis to ensure that there are not systematic differences between the students participating in the alternative experiences.

Challenges

For teaching and counseling faculty, the biggest challenge has been finding time for both course content and success skills topics. The faculty who integrated success skills into course content rather than introducing success skills as a separate topic have reported the greatest satisfaction with the approach.

A Commitment To Using Data

Building on the college's commitment to data-informed work, both teaching and counseling faculty have supported *Counselor-Enhanced Developmental Learning Communities* and have insisted that program development and continuation be grounded in data. Thus, program results continually increase faculty members' understanding of the relationship between counseling-enhanced developmental classes and student success, informing curricular design and resource allocation.

In fall 2010, Skagit leaders decided to administer *SENSE* to obtain more targeted information about students new to the college. As a result, Skagit expanded the *Learning Communities Program* to include Adult Basic Education (ABE) counselor-enhanced classes and college-level learning communities that specifically target first-year students. Through *SENSE*, college leaders learned that while 72% of entering students may be aware of writing, math, or other skill labs to help with their coursework, 62% never used them. To close this gap, the college expanded professional development activities that focus on teaching strategies that encourage further integration of classroom and skill lab activities.

Partnerships To Strengthen College Readiness
El Paso Community College (TX)

Established in 1969, El Paso Community College (EPCC) serves nearly 30,000 students at five campuses and three training centers. The student population is primarily Hispanic, and a majority of students are the first in their families to attend college. EPCC is one of the original members of Achieving the Dream and has implemented a broad array of initiatives to improve student success.

EPCC has taken the lead in launching initiatives that help students prepare for college, focusing its efforts on students still in high school, as well as older students who are preparing to come to college for the first time.

The college has a history of partnering across the education system: Students who enroll at the community college are simultaneously enrolled at the University of Texas at El Paso (UTEP), with no barriers to articulation or transfer. Reaching out in the other direction, the college engages in a collaborative initiative with area high schools to increase college readiness among high school students and thus reduce the need for developmental coursework.

Helping Students Become College-Ready

Driven by data showing that 98% of area high school students placed into at least one developmental math, reading, or writing course, the college entered into the *College Readiness Initiative,* a joint project with UTEP and 12 area school districts. According to college leaders, their first goal was to get high school students college-ready before they graduated so when they came to EPCC or UTEP they would not have to go through the developmental sequence. A second goal, for students who still needed developmental education coursework, was to decrease the amount of time required for completion of the developmental sequence. EPCC administrators and faculty thought it would be possible to accelerate student progress through developmental classes so students could start earning college credit hours as quickly as possible.

The first pilot of the *College Readiness Initiative* began in the spring of 2006 with 4,000 students from six local high schools. The program is conducted at the high schools and includes a comprehensive orientation on ACCUPLACER (the college's placement test) for students and their parents, followed by testing during a student's junior and/or senior years in high school. Counselors review scores with students: Those who do not pass all areas of the placement test work on refreshing their skills and are then retested. By 2007, the program expanded to serve nearly 10,000 students. All 12 area high schools now are involved.

Showing Results in the College Readiness Initiative

Since the *College Readiness* protocol was established, fewer EPCC students have placed into developmental courses. After the first year, students who scored in the college-ready range on the ACCUPLACER assessment increased from 3% to 5 % in math, from 30% to 35% in reading, and from 51% to 66 % in writing. Those who placed into the lowest level of developmental math decreased from 31% to 22%. Students who placed into the highest level of developmental math increased from 28% to 41%.

Creating College-High School Partnerships

The success of the *College Readiness Initiative* hinges on cooperation among 12 independent high school districts, a community college, and a university. High school leaders credit the community college with initiating the conversation with high school superintendents. Rather than looking for someone to blame for entering students' lack of college readiness, community college leaders shared the data and asked the question, "Okay, what do we do?" The initial meeting between high school and college leaders led to creation of a consortium to work collaboratively and share student data. The consortium is co-chaired by the EPCC vice president of instruction and the UTEP provost. The colleges jointly fund a college readiness director and a college readiness researcher.

Improving Basic Skills in a Summer Bridge Program

EPCC does not end its work with high school students when they graduate. Part of the *College Readiness Initiative*, *Summer Bridge* program strives to improve students' basic skills in reading, writing, and math through tutoring and a three-credit summer course. Students learn about college resources and how to develop college success strategies such as positive motivation, decision-making, and self-direction. In addition, they have the opportunity to retake the college placement test. Ninety-seven percent of students who complete *Summer Bridge* subsequently enroll for the fall semester at either EPCC or UTEP.

PREP: Pre-testing, Retesting Education Program

Realizing that EPCC serves a large adult population who either graduated from high school a long time ago or did not graduate at all, the college launched the *PREP* initiative. *PREP's* goal is similar to the *College Readiness Initiative* — to get students college-ready or get them placed as high as possible in the developmental course sequence so they have fewer developmental courses to take before they can earn college credit. Funded by Title V, *PREP* is aimed at improving student preparation and persistence in higher education through a case-management approach. *PREP* specialists assist entering students in understanding the significance of the college placement test, developing an individualized preparation program, and refreshing basic skills. A variety of factors are considered, including the student's prior education and grades, the length of time since the student was last enrolled in an academic setting, and the choice of degree plan and career. Specialists also follow up with students to make sure they are on track.

Showing Results in PREP

In the 2007–08 school year, 2,510 students were served by *PREP*. They showed significant success in progressing at least one course level on the placement test: Fifty-seven percent progressed in math, 58% in reading, and 64% in writing. Testing through the *PREP* initiative had an unanticipated outcome of increasing college awareness and participation: More students subsequently enrolled at either EPCC or UTEP.

Next Steps

Realizing there is more work to be done, the college created *Start Right*, a mini-think tank made up of faculty, staff, and students. College leaders refer to *Start Right* as their "engine for moving new ideas."

Connecting with First-Time Students
Sacramento City College (CA)

Sacramento City College (SCC) serves the greater Sacramento, CA, area, with a main city campus and two additional centers in West Sacramento and Davis. Founded in 1916 as a department of Sacramento High School, the community college now is part of the Los Rios Community College District. Enrollment is approximately 25,000 students, including recent increases in the numbers of first-time freshmen.

Creating a Culture of Evidence

In 2006, newly hired college leaders analyzed existing data, asking themselves, "What are we missing? Where are the gaps? What do students need to be successful?" They collected more information about students' experiences at the college through focus groups and surveys of student engagement and satisfaction. They set out to develop a culture of evidence by using data regularly to make decisions about programs and services for students.

Through their data collection, college leaders learned that often their new students felt disconnected and even scared. As a result, they designed an array of initiatives to help students navigate the pathways through the enrollment process and to take the fear and intimidation out of the entering student experience.

Sending the Right Message

SCC leaders recognized the need to communicate clear and consistent messages to students. Information posted throughout the campus reminds students what is expected of them and points them to the help available. Signs and website banners remind students to check their financial aid status, pay enrollment fees to avoid automatically being dropped from classes, and seek counseling to develop an academic plan. Communication also focuses on advising and early registration dates.

Targeting Incoming Freshmen

Reaching out to high school seniors and their parents, SCC established *Senior Saturday* events in the spring. Prospective students take placement tests, attend orientation, become familiar with campus services and student organizations, and learn about financial aid.

Students Obtaining Success (SOS)

When students first contact the college, they receive a letter with step-by-step instructions for college entry, from admissions and mandatory information sessions to placement testing, counseling workshops, applying for financial aid, and registering for classes. Following up with incoming students, college leaders learned that because they were provided with an explicit description of steps in the registration process, students said the campus seemed comfortable from the first day they arrived.

Responding to student requests for more guidance as they prepared to start classes, the college added a half-day workshop, *Getting Ready for the First Week*. In the workshop, students learn the basics about their first days in college: Remember to bring a pencil and a schedule to class the first day, find classrooms before the semester starts, go to the bookstore, and visit the financial aid lab. Four hundred out of 2,000 incoming freshmen signed up for the workshop the first time it was offered. Students then asked if the college would offer a similar program mid-semester to make sure they are on track.

The Personal Touch

When the college's research showed that new students did not feel welcome, the college staffed all campus and building entrances with administrators, faculty, and staff to personally greet students at the beginning of the semester. Front-line staff and faculty received training in *SOS*, leading to an increased understanding of the student experience and more seamless service across departments.

411 for Success

Learning from students that they did not really know what they were expected to do week-by-week once they started classes, SCC launched *411 for Success* — a website and a collection of handouts that feature week-by-week mini-tutorials on such subjects as when to drop classes and when to touch base with professors. In the first four months, the website received 25,000 hits. For instant access to the site, students are able to scan a QR code with their smart phones.

One-Stop Shopping

In line with SCC's focus on streamlining and simplifying the entering student process, the college combined key campus services into a centralized Financial Aid/Registration Laboratory. The one-stop approach also is available to students online and includes a full array of services important to the entering student, including college application, registration, financial aid assistance, FAFSA workshops, and student success workshops.

Showing Progress

After five years of building out initiatives focused on the entering student, SCC is seeing results. Students are changing their behaviors in ways that promote their own success while also meeting the college's expectations. Seventy percent of students are registering earlier than they did before. Students are applying earlier for financial aid, and 90% of eligible students are receiving it well before classes begin. In the past, as many as 7,000 students each semester were dropped for non-payment of tuition simply because they missed deadlines. That number has dropped to between 100 and 200 students each semester. In addition, the college's various support centers are packed with students who are aware of and eager to take advantage of services available to them. Students from ages 18–20 demonstrated increasing course success rates over the past several years. The course success rate of recent high school graduates also has been increasing and now exceeds that of all other students. The fall-to-spring persistence rate of recent high school graduates increased steadily from the 2006–07 academic year to the 2009–10 academic year before falling slightly for 2010–11, when major budget cuts affected some first-year course offerings. Students now are asking college leaders to make student participation in many of these initiatives mandatory.

College leaders say they put together this collection of strategies "to show our students that we care" in the hope that the approach would prompt students to change their behaviors. As one leader put it, "It is important to offer them reminders and let them know they are not just a number but a member of our campus community."

Focusing on the First Year
Zane State College (OH)

Located in Zanesville, OH, in the southeastern part of the state, Zane State College serves approximately 2,900 students. An Achieving the Dream college, the institution consistently has performed well, relative to other institutions, on *CCSSE's* student engagement benchmarks. Zane State's success at engaging first-year students cannot be attributed to a single program or strategy. Clearly, students are responding to a combination of initiatives, underscored by an explicit collegewide commitment to developing relationships with students.

The Personal Touch

The college is committed to making personal connections and building relationships with students to help them succeed. College leaders introduced a core philosophy, *Personal Touch – Respect, Responsibility, and Responsiveness,* which is built into every initiative, undergirding everything the college does. *Personal Touch* is embedded in the mission statement, integrated into orientation and professional development activities, and enacted by individual faculty and staff members.

FIT for Success — The First-Year Experience

In 2006, Zane State participated in the Foundations of Excellence self-study and audit of the first-year experience. As a result, a team of faculty, staff, and students developed *FIT for Success: Finding Inspiration Together*. Three principles guided the team: building on the *Personal Touch* philosophy, recognizing that the first year begins not on the first day of classes but at the first point of contact with students, and speaking to differences between first-year and second-year students.

Many of Zane State's students are the first in their families to attend college. They have little experience to help them navigate higher education systems and overcome challenges that arise. In addition, many Zane State students are from low-income backgrounds and often may be more focused on developing immediate survival skills than on thinking about their future and potential for achievement. College leaders therefore recognize the need to understand these circumstances and then to connect teaching methods and college services to students' experiences and values.

Making It Mandatory

The college introduced mandatory experiences for the nearly 1,000 new students who enter each year. All entering students are now required to take placement tests and to attend a new-student orientation. A mandatory first-year experience course was associated with a 10% increase in fall-to-fall student persistence during its first year of implementation. The course is offered in a variety of formats, including on-campus and online, to meet the needs of students.

Intrusive Advising

Zane State implemented intrusive advising to help at-risk and underprepared students succeed. Designed to foster personal connections with students, the intrusive advising activities include personal phone calls, mandatory meetings, emails, and Facebook postings. This ongoing interaction has made it possible for advisors to remind students of peer and professional tutoring, writing workshops, and other services available to them.

Increasing Math Placement Scores and Success

The *Math Start* program requires that students who test two levels below college math complete at least the first developmental math course within their first three academic quarters at the college. A no-cost skills workshop helps students to review and improve their math skills, using a customized curriculum. On average, nine out of 10 students who complete the workshop place at least one level higher in the developmental course sequence than their original placement, with one in four placing into college-level math.

Showing Results

The combination of first-year initiatives is paying off. Fall-to-fall persistence of those students deemed most at risk has increased by a range of 10% to 16% each year over the 2006 baseline data — with each of the most recent two cohort groups performing as well as or better than their less at-risk peers. At the same time, the percentage of students successfully completing all required developmental education courses within the first year of enrollment has increased by 20% in reading, 20% in English, and 10% in math. Overall, the college's fall-to-fall retention improved by 6% and at even higher rates for sub-groups of the student population: Fall-to-fall persistence of part-time students increased by 24%; for male students, by 11%; and for students between the ages of 20 and 24, by 13%.

As a result of these efforts, including college policies of mandatory testing, mandatory placement, mandatory orientation, and a mandatory first-year experience course, students beginning in developmental education are achieving on-time graduation rates. The three-year graduation rate for developmental students now exceeds 50%. In fact, 87% of students who successfully complete the first year at Zane State and return the next fall are able to complete their degrees within three years, whether or not they began in developmental education.

GPS for Student Success
Century College (MN)

Century College serves 11,000 students at a suburban campus in White Bear Lake, MN. It is one of several community colleges in the Minneapolis-St. Paul area.

Streamlining Support for New Students

As at many community colleges, leaders at Century were looking for ways to increase entering students' persistence rates, especially for those who test into developmental education courses. Inspired by the results of efforts to strengthen and streamline services for entering students at Valencia College (FL), Century's counseling staff looked at Valencia's *LifeMap* concept. They then began to explore what could be done at Century and other Minnesota community colleges to promote stronger connections among new students, faculty, and staff and to strengthen support services for students through improved organization, coordination, communication, and delivery.

Intentional Connections through GPS LifePlan

An advisory team comprising faculty, staff, and administrators from community colleges in the Minnesota State College and Universities system created a comprehensive program that could be customized to the needs of each college. The team developed the *GPS (Goals+Plans = Success) LifePlan,* which provides a framework to help students set goals and make educational, personal, financial, career, and leadership plans. Members of the team believed that students would benefit from having services and information resources organized and in one place. With student affairs and academic affairs staff working in partnership, they designed a way to build *GPS LifePlan* into the curriculum.

GPS LifePlan made its campus debut in spring 2006, connecting students to the faculty, information resources, and services needed to help them achieve their goals. The program contains three components: a one-stop website (www.gpslifeplan.org/century) that outlines the five areas of goal setting, with links to resources and activities; a student-owned virtual portfolio (eFolio) that helps organize materials and track progress; and campus workshops and events that help students develop particular skills.

There are 70 lesson plans to help instructors incorporate aspects of *GPS LifePlan* into the curriculum. For example, an English class might focus on financial goals by having students write essays for scholarships; a class in dental hygiene might include helping students focus on career goals. Empowering faculty to use *GPS LifePlan* in the classroom has advanced the objective of ensuring that it is fully integrated into students' educational experiences.

Collaboration and Faculty Ownership

To ensure that *GPS LifePlan* would be seen as broader than a student services initiative, Century leaders say it was important to invite faculty members to become an integral part of the process. They have been involved as advisors, as well as in the classroom. Encouraged to use the program in the college curriculum, faculty members were able to take ownership of the effort. Faculty members involved in the program have received recognition for their work and a small stipend for developing lesson plans and assignments. College leaders say this approach built support across the college and contributed to early adoption of the program. A large proportion of Century faculty members now are actively involved with *GPS LifePlan,* working with students and building it into class assignments.

Showing Results

From the beginning, leaders of the initiative incorporated internal evaluation, including a survey of faculty and students. In 2007, an external evaluator conducted a more comprehensive review. Results indicated that entering first-time students' fall-to-fall persistence increased significantly (from 59.5% to 64%) after the first full year of *GPS LifePlan* implementation. A more structured and intense application of *GPS LifePlan* with a developmental reading cohort showed an increase in fall-to-spring student persistence to 76.9%, compared to an average of 65.8% for previous years. There was also a corresponding decrease in course withdrawal rates and an improvement in final course grades.

The promising early results have continued, as recent fall-to-spring persistence rates for full-time students using *GPS LifePlan* were at 81%, compared to 72% for other students.

Along with increases in student persistence, Century also has seen significant increases in *CCSSE* benchmark scores for Student-Faculty Interaction and Support for Learners. While these scores reflect the effects of a collection of student success initiatives, many of the initiatives, including a new student seminar and student success advising, have incorporated *GPS LifePlan.*

Becoming Part of the College Culture

Early collaboration among departments on each campus and within the larger state system has reaped multiple benefits. By working together, collaborators broke down the divisions between areas and saw the value of developing a common language. In addition, both faculty and administrators were involved at each stage of creating and maintaining the program. A faculty communication workgroup continued to examine the specific needs and concerns that faculty might have with the development of such a comprehensive program.

In addition to consistent faculty input, an advisory panel of faculty, staff, and administrators from the Minnesota State Colleges and Universities system continues to meet monthly to focus on *GPS LifePlan* use in the classroom and other areas of student engagement. And, most significantly, the initial goal of the project is being realized — students are benefiting significantly from *GPS LifePlan.* College leaders attribute the success of *GPS LifePlan* to actively acknowledging the reality of college life for their students and providing tools that help them set realistic goals at the beginning of their college experience.

A Statewide Strategy To Create a College-Going Culture
Virginia Community College System

While many innovative and effective practices start on a single community college campus, two promising practices — the *Career Coach Program* and the online *Virginia Wizard* — were initiated at the Virginia Community College System (VCCS).

System leaders recognized that high school counselors pressed for time tend to focus on the needs of the top and bottom 10% of students, leaving the middle majority with inadequate attention. These students, the likely mainstay of Virginia's emerging workforce, were graduating from high school in large numbers without career goals or plans for postsecondary education or training.

Career Coach Program

In fall 2005, the VCCS launched a *Career Coach Program* that placed community college personnel in local high schools to help students make informed decisions about college opportunities and careers. The goal was to convince all high school students that the 12th grade is not the finish line.

Key components of the program include facilitating the development of individual career plans and portfolios; administering and interpreting career assessments; providing information on careers and career pathways; connecting students to early college programs; and easing the transition from high school to postsecondary education, training, and the skilled workforce.

Virginia Western Community College Adopts Career Coach Program

One college that quickly embraced the new initiative was Virginia Western Community College, which serves more than 8,700 credit students in a six-county region with a main campus in Roanoke, off-campus classes, and two extension centers.

In the first year, the college placed three coaches in local schools, working with about 500 students. The coaches are part-time college employees from a range of backgrounds, typically working 25 hours per week.

Collaboration

At first, the *Career Coach Program* encountered a mixed reception. Some high school administrators were very concerned, not knowing what the coaches would do. But Virginia Western had good relationships with their local schools and worked to build trust. The coaches create relationships with high school principals, guidance counselors, and teachers. They speak to students in classes and at campus events, as well as meet with students individually and in small groups.

The community college career coaches will work with any student, whether the individual wants to transfer to the university to major in history, or to go into the military, or to learn welding. They help students with the information needed to make decisions for themselves. Increasingly, the counselors and teachers at the high schools have referred students to the career coaches, and students themselves began encouraging their friends to work with the Virginia Western career coaches.

Currently there are six Virginia Western career coaches serving in nine of the college's 15 feeder schools. Most high school administrators have become receptive to the idea of the coaches because they see the significant value of these added resources in their schools.

Showing Results

During the 2010–11 school year, career coaches serving in 180 high schools across Virginia provided individual or small group coaching to more than 38,000 students. As a result of working with a career coach, more than 19,000 students developed written academic and career plans.

Evaluation data show that students give high marks to career coaching. Similarly, 95% of high school principals indicate they are very satisfied and that the coaches have met or exceeded their expectations. While the coaches promote all higher education options, community colleges are enrolling a much higher percentage of recent high school graduates than they did before. Statewide, 9,500 recent high school students who had worked with career coaches graduated from high school and enrolled in community colleges.

Virginia Wizard

A second statewide initiative, the *Virginia Wizard*, was developed collaboratively to complement the *Career Coach Program*. The web-based resource provides powerful assessment tools, including a range of interest, skills, and aptitude inventories. As early as the 8th and 9th grades, students are encouraged to take individualized assessments, which help them develop a personalized academic and career plan and identify what courses, certificates, or degrees are required in their fields of interest. The Wizard identifies academic and articulation programs at state colleges and universities, and it also reports typical salaries and demand for various careers in the local employment region.

CHAPTER 9

Listening, Learning, Acting

Throughout this book, we have listened. From student voices, we have learned new things. We have perhaps confirmed things we thought we already knew. We have heard soft voices confirm hard data. And we certainly have had some fondly held notions about community college students challenged or even flatly refuted. We have been inspired, and we have been dismayed.

Now what?

This final chapter offers observations about potential next steps for community colleges. It is not a guide for transformational change in institutions, though hopefully it will be pertinent in addressing that challenge. It is not a delineation of a student success agenda, though it will inform that work. It is not a leadership primer, though leadership for student success is clearly critical. Rather, the following pages offer continuing encouragement to listen to student voices, with observations about how to *listen well,* lessons about the power of institutional culture that emerge from the work of listening, and an emerging set of "design principles" that will determine the quality of implementation of the kinds of educational experiences that students say are important to them.

On Listening Well

Since 2002, the Center has conducted more than 200 focus groups and interviews with currently enrolled students, prospective students, those who are close to graduating or transferring to a university, those who have already graduated, individuals who have dropped out of college, and high school seniors anticipating college. Taken separately, each person's description of his or her educational experiences represents one person's story — an anecdote, an interesting tale woven of recollections and reflections. But collectively, these stories add up to much more. Themes emerge. Similarities and differences in experiences become clear. For the community college practitioner, the collective student story points to a college's strengths and those areas of practice needing improvement. Sanford "Sandy" Shugart, president of Valencia College, says it well: "College is what students experience." As a complement to each college's data on student learning, progress, and attainment, the student voice provides a roadmap for institutional action.

In addition to an institution's quantitative data collection, including routine student cohort tracking and participation in *CCSSE, SENSE,* CCIS, and other national and statewide projects, community colleges make significant discoveries by listening to their own students through focus groups. To help colleges establish the capacity for learning from student focus groups, the Center provides a free online focus group toolkit containing guidelines and tools that can be locally adapted.[1] Components of the toolkit also are included in the DVD accompanying this book.

Briefly described below are lessons learned from a decade of encouraging students to speak while we listen.

Listen systematically.

An essential element is determining what the college wants to learn from students and how the information they provide will be used. (Data rule: Never collect data until it is clear who, by name, will use what data and for what purposes.) This is more easily said than done and is the foundational work most often skipped.

Typically, it is useful to begin with thoughtful examination and discussion of the quantitative data from cohort tracking and surveys, identifying areas where students succeed, stumble, or stop. Then it is possible to ask, "What else do we need to know to understand more deeply what our students are experiencing?" "In what areas of institutional performance are students our best — or only — informants?" "From which student groups do we particularly need to hear?" "How should we prioritize our 'needs for knowing?'"

The next step is to develop a focus group protocol — a set of discussion categories and questions to be asked of all students. Random, scattered conversations lead nowhere. Hearing responses to consistent questions from a number of students will provide actionable information. And more often than not, it also will lead to more questions! The culture of inquiry thus created should be a quintessential characteristic of community colleges on a mission to promote student success.

Listen to students who reflect the college's student population.

The student body president and other student leaders might be seen as formally representing the students at a college; in a democratic sense, they do. However, they do not represent the student voice on the campus. They represent one group of students — those who are engaged in particular ways beyond the classroom. The objective is not to hear from *special* students but to hear from *typical* students — students who are engaged, as well as those who are not. If focus groups involve only one type of student — nursing students, TRIO participants, developmental education students, or student leaders — then facilitators will hear only a limited slice of students' experience. And there will be no way to know whether that slice differs from other students' experiences. A student in the nursing program has a significantly different experience from the individual who has not yet declared a major and is moving through the developmental course sequence. It is important to hear from both. It is important to hear from students who reflect different groups within the student population: men and women, white students and students of color, part-time and full-time students, entering students and experienced students, day-time and evening students, athletes and future founders of technology companies, the well-prepared and the underprepared, the affluent and the poor, those who came to college immediately after graduating from high school and those who returned to college after years in the workforce. The students who truly represent the diverse students the college serves will tell us what we need to hear.

Obviously, it is not possible to listen to everyone at once, but it is possible to pursue the goal of listening broadly over time. There are times, too, when a college has a specific need to focus on a particular subpopulation of students. For example, a college may wish to understand more fully why men of color are dropping out at disproportionately high rates. But even focus groups involving only men of color need ultimately to encompass a range of individuals, representing differences in age, major, educational background, and so on. And a sound understanding of student experiences will require an exploration of whether, and in what ways, the experiences of men of color differ from those of women of color, or white men, or all other students.

Be prepared to hear what you do not want to hear.

When college faculty, staff, and administrators hear their students describe experiences at the college, at times they will want to cheer and at times they will want to weep. Of course, they must do neither — at least not in the midst of a focus group session. A commitment to improving outcomes for more students brings the necessity of learning which college practices are working for students and which are not. If the disposition is to invite only students who will tell us what we want to hear, then we inevitably hear only part of the story. What are the strengths students see in the college? What types of learning environments motivate them to attend class and do their academic work? What messages do they hear from faculty and staff about themselves, as students and as individual human beings? What types of learning environments turn them off? What experiences cause frustration for them? Why aren't they using the services provided by the college? What makes them walk away? What steps do they believe the college should take to help more students succeed? College leaders at all levels need to hear all of it to understand what the college's next steps should be.

Listen past backward baseball caps.

The work of the Center includes videotaping focus groups (with students' permission) to bring the student voice to community colleges throughout the country. Very early in the work, the Center provided guidelines for focus group participants with instructions on appropriate dress for the camera, so that students' appearance would not distract from what they were saying. Soon the guidelines hit the trash can. Students' backward baseball caps, headscarves, low-hanging jeans, tattoos, and piercings are the outer layers that sometimes distract adult professionals from all the wisdom, strength, and honesty students bring to the focus group and to their college journey. To listen well, we must not permit ourselves to be distracted by the outer layers. Regardless of their style choices, students' voices tell the truth about their college experiences.

Enter the room assuming you know nothing.

Perhaps the greatest challenge for colleges in conducting their own focus groups is to ensure that facilitators are trained to be blank slates. To be sure, they have come prepared with a clearly organized protocol for the conversation with students. As researchers, they may have certain hypotheses in mind. But they must not come to a focus group with answers embedded in their questions, or with nonverbal communication that transmits disapproval, encouragement, doubt, or fervent belief. What is important, of course, is *listening hard* — and being interested and curious enough to follow up — to say, "Please tell us more about that." What is important is actually learning from what students tell us.

Students are waiting to be asked. *Listen well.*

It Is All about College Culture

A truly remarkable thing happens when you visit a college campus for the first time and begin encountering people. You run into security officers in the parking lot, maintenance workers and other staff as you look for your destination, faculty and staff in both formal and informal settings. You meet students — sometimes driving your cab from the airport or checking you in at the hotel, sometimes in the student center or the restroom, and then in the focus group session. And what happens in very short order is that the culture of the college becomes strikingly evident. Organizational culture — often defined as "the way we do things around here" — is a multifaceted thing, of course. Five desirable dimensions of culture emerge from a decade of listening tours in American community colleges.

A Culture of Connection

Some community colleges clearly have established a culture of connection in which relationships are valued and intentionally nurtured. The counterpoint appears to be a culture of alienation, in which students and others experience themselves as set apart, left out, and unaccompanied on the educational journey.

A Culture of High Expectations

Vincent Tinto, distinguished university professor at Syracuse University and long-time scholar of student retention, often and correctly observes that "no one rises to low expectations." There could be no clearer lesson from students than that. While they say they appreciate the times the college works with them to manage their competing priorities (a sick child, a job shift change), they also clearly know when faculty and others hold low expectations for their performance. And they hate it.

A Culture of Potential

Quickly evident to a careful listener is the language that college faculty and staff use to describe their students. The language is never neutral. Typically it tends toward descriptions either of student deficiencies or of student assets, students as victims or students as heroes.

A Culture of Collaboration

As is often noted in the literature on student retention and success, students are whole human beings. They do not have an academic division and a student services division in their heads; neither, for that matter, do they have a reading department and a psychology department. They are thinking and emotional beings. Colleges that are listening to their students are finding that collaboration across divisions and disciplines, and integration of academic support with instruction, serve students well. Further, the value of student-to-student collaboration figures strongly in effective teaching and learning, and colleges listening to their students are making collaborative learning a hallmark of their institutions.

A Culture of Evidence and Inquiry

As previously noted, student focus groups and interviews are but one of several important tools for learning about students and figuring out how the college can more effectively support their learning and progression. Further, *gathering* data, whether from cohort tracking, engagement surveys, program evaluation, or other sources, is but the first step. Data quality is important, of course. But the truly transformational opportunities come when the people of the college are broadly engaged in *understanding* the data, *using* the data to paint an honest picture of their students' educational experiences, and then *applying* the data in redesigning those experiences for better results. We cannot get better at what we are not willing to look at.

Changing Culture

Culture is a virus. Time and time again the listener finds that the values and assumptions predominating among faculty are also found among students, that the tone set by governing boards and presidents makes a significant difference across the college community. Positive or negative, culture pervades. It can be changed but only with intentionality, diligence, and collective effort. The good news is that most of the work costs nothing.

Still, changing culture is perhaps the most difficult work of a student success agenda. Michael Fullan, a well-known author on change in education, talks about "re-culturing" as a central challenge:

> *"We tend to meet any situation by reorganizing. What a wonderful method this can be for creating the illusion of progress, while producing confusion, inefficiency, and demoralization. Structure does make a difference, but it is not the main point of achieving success. Transforming the culture — changing the way we do things around here — is the main point. I call this re-culturing."*[2]

Design Principles for Effective Educational Practice

Listening to students inevitably involves hearing from them about specific educational practices — both policies and programs — that either help or hinder their success, optimize their experience, or waste their time. More broadly, the community college field, including the Center and many other organizations and individuals, is intensively involved in work to identify and promote effective educational practice. Still, it is important that the local and national student success agendas not devolve into an oversimplified list of must-do practices or an innovation arms race. Addressing cultural change, Fullan asserts:

"Leading in a culture of change means creating a culture (not just a structure) of change. It does not mean adopting innovations, one after another; it does mean producing the capacity to seek, critically assess, and selectively incorporate new ideas and practices — all the time, inside the organization as well as outside it."[3]

So, while continuing to seek evidence of what works for students and wisdom about leadership for change, we also seek understanding of the qualities typically embedded in effective practices. These shared features can be used as design principles in restructuring students' educational experience. The point is not to *innovate* the most but to *design* the best — which includes diligence in regard to the *quality of implementation* of whatever practices colleges may choose to deploy. The following design principles, originally presented in the Center's report *A Matter of Degrees*,[4] provide a useful beginning as colleges seek to apply what they learn by listening:

A Strong Start

Focusing attention on the front door of the college — ensuring that students' earliest contacts and first weeks incorporate experiences that will foster personal connections and enhance their chances of success — is a smart investment.

Clear, Coherent Pathways

The many choices and options students face as they endeavor to navigate through college systems can create unnecessary confusion — and inhibit students' success. Colleges can improve student success (and minimize ill-used time) by creating coherent pathways that help students move through an engaging collegiate experience.

Integrated Support

A large part of improving success involves effectively connecting with students where they are most likely to be: in the classroom. This means building support, such as skills development and supplemental instruction, into coursework rather than referring students to services that are separate from the learning experience.

High Expectations and High Support

Students do their best when the bar is high but within reach. Setting a high standard and then giving students the necessary support — academic planning, academic support, financial aid, and so on — makes the standard attainable.

Intensive Student Engagement

Promoting student engagement is the overarching feature of successful program design, and all other features support it. In design and implementation of the collegiate experience, colleges must make engagement inescapable for their students.

Design for Scale

Bringing practices to scale requires a long-term commitment of time and money. Securing and maintaining this commitment requires significant political, financial, and human capital. In addition to allocating — and reallocating — available funding, colleges must genuinely involve faculty, staff, and students.

Professional Development

Improving student success rates and meeting college completion goals require individuals not only to re-conceptualize their roles but also to work differently. This means that professional development is not just for instructors. It is for everyone: staff, faculty, administrators, and governing boards.

Doing More of What We Know Works

Researchers, being researchers, will continue to press hard for high-quality evidence of effective educational practice in community colleges. In the meantime, though, colleges are losing students at an unacceptably high rate, and those students' lives will be dramatically affected. Also in the meantime, practitioners *know enough* to create quite different and much more effective educational experiences for their students. Deborah Meier, a MacArthur Fellow and highly acclaimed leader in American education reform, captures reality in this way: "It's not that we're ignorant and don't know what to do. The question is whether we want to do it badly enough."[5]

And so we hear the echoes of student voices in our hallways and in our heads. We know what to do.

Are we listening?

Endnotes, References, and Resources

Endnotes

Introduction. Lifting Up the Student Voice

1 Staklis, S., & Chen, X. (2010). *Profile of undergraduate students: Trends from selected years, 1995–96 to 2007–08* (NCES 2010-220). Washington, DC: National Center for Education Statistics, Institute of Education Sciences, U.S. Department of Education. Retrieved from http://nces.ed.gov/pubs2010/2010220.pdf

2 *Ibid.*

3 *Ibid.*

4 Hussar, W. J., & Bailey, T. M. (2011). *Projections of education statistics to 2019* (NCES 2011-017). Washington, DC: National Center for Education Statistics, Institute of Education Sciences, U.S. Department of Education.

5 Staklis, S., & Chen, X. (2010). *Profile of undergraduate students: Trends from selected years, 1995–96 to 2007–08* (NCES 2010-220). Washington, DC: National Center for Education Statistics, Institute of Education Sciences, U.S. Department of Education. Retrieved from http://nces.ed.gov/pubs2010/2010220.pdf

6 U.S. Department of Education. 2009 Integrated Postsecondary Education Data System (IPEDS). Washington, DC: National Center for Education Statistics. Retrieved from http://nces.ed.gov

7 Jones, D. P., & Ewell, P. T. (2009). *Utilizing college access & completion innovation funds to improve postsecondary attainment in California*. Boulder, CO: National Center for Higher Education Management Systems.

8 Snyder, T. D., & Dillow, S. A. (2011). *Digest of education statistics, 2010* (NCES 2011-015). Washington, DC: National Center for Education Statistics, Institute of Education Sciences, U.S. Department of Education.

9 To enhance readability, we have occasionally deleted some extraneous language in students' quotes without changing their intended meaning.

Chapter 2. Ready or Not

1 Bressoud, D. (2012). *Why is the transition from high school to college important? Issues and next steps.* Paper presented at the Joint Math Meetings, Boston, MA. Retrieved from http://www.macalester.edu/~bressoud/talks/2012/MAA-NCTM.pdf

2 Adelman, C. (2004). *Principal indicators of student academic histories in postsecondary education, 1972–2000*. Washington, DC: Institute of Education Sciences, U.S. Department of Education.

Chapter 4. First Steps on the Pathway

1 Jenkins, D., & Cho, S. (2012). *Get with the program: Accelerating community college students' entry into and completion of programs of study* (CCRC Working Paper No. 32). New York, NY: Columbia University, Teachers College, Community College Research Center.

2 Jenkins, D., & Weiss, M. J. (2011). *Charting pathways to completion for low-income community college students* (CCRC Working Paper No. 34). New York, NY: Columbia University, Teachers College, Community College Research Center.

Chapter 7. Disengaging: Now You See Me, Now You Don't

1 Berkner, L., & Choy, S. (2008). *Descriptive summary of 2003–04 beginning postsecondary students: Three years later* (NCES 2008-174). Washington, DC: National Center for Education Statistics, Institute of Education Sciences, U.S. Department of Education.

2 Radford, A. W., Berkner, L., Wheeless, S. C., & Shepherd, B. (2010). *Persistence and attainment of 2003–04 beginning postsecondary students: After 6 years* (NCES 2011-151). Washington, DC: National Center for Education Statistics, Institute of Education Sciences, U.S. Department of Education. Retrieved from http://nces.ed.gov/pubs2011/2011151.pdf

3 *Ibid.*

4 Jenkins, D., & Weiss, M. J. (2011). *Charting pathways to completion for low-income community college students* (CCRC Working Paper No. 34). New York, NY: Columbia University, Teachers College, Community College Research Center.

Chapter 8. Community Colleges: Doing What Works for Students

1 Center for Community College Student Engagement *(CCCSE)*. (2012). *A matter of degrees: Promising practices for community college student success (A first look)*. Austin, TX: University of Texas at Austin, Community College Leadership Program.

Chapter 9. Listening, Learning, Acting

1 Center for Community College Student Engagement *(CCCSE)*. (2012). *Focus group toolkit*. Austin, TX: University of Texas at Austin, Community College Leadership Program. Retrieved from http://www.ccsse.org/center/iss/focusgrouptoolkit.cfm

2 Fullan, M. (2001). *Leading in a culture of change*. San Francisco, CA: Jossey-Bass.

3 *Ibid.*

4 Center for Community College Student Engagement *(CCCSE)*. (2012). *A matter of degrees: Promising practices for community college student success (A first look)*. Austin, TX: University of Texas at Austin, Community College Leadership Program, p. 5.

5 Meier, D. (1993). Personal communication.

References

Introduction. Lifting Up the Student Voice

Adelman, C. (2004). *Principal indicators of student academic histories in postsecondary education,1972–2000.* Washington, DC: Institute of Education Sciences, U.S. Department of Education.

Bailey, T., Alfonso, M., Calcagno, J. C., Jenkins, D., Kienzl, G., & Leinbach, T. (2004). *Improving student attainment in community colleges: Institutional characteristics and policies.* New York, NY: Columbia University, Teachers College, Community College Research Center.

Center for Community College Student Engagement *(CCCSE).* (2010). *The heart of student success: Teaching, learning, and college completion (2010 CCCSE findings).* Austin, TX: University of Texas at Austin, Community College Leadership Program.

Center for Community College Student Engagement *(CCCSE).* (2012). *A matter of degrees: Promising practices for community college student success (A first look).* Austin, TX: University of Texas at Austin, Community College Leadership Program.

Gawande, A. (2010). *The checklist manifesto: How to get things right.* New York, NY: Metropolitan Books.

Hussar, W. J., & Bailey, T. M. (2011). *Projections of education statistics to 2019* (NCES 2011-017). Washington, DC: National Center for Education Statistics, Institute of Education Sciences, U.S. Department of Education.

Jones, D. P., & Ewell, P. T. (2009). *Utilizing college access & completion innovation funds to improve postsecondary attainment in California.* Boulder, CO: National Center for Higher Education Management Systems.

Kojaku, L. K., & Nunez, A. M. (1998). *Descriptive summary of 1995–1996 beginning postsecondary students: With profiles of students entering 2- and 4-year institutions* (NCES 1999-030). Washington, DC: National Center for Education Statistics, U.S. Department of Education.

Mullin, C. M. (2010). *Rebalancing the mission: The community college completion challenge* (Policy Brief 2010-02PBL). Washington, DC: American Association of Community Colleges.

Snyder, T. D., & Dillow, S. A. (2011). *Digest of education statistics, 2010* (NCES 2011-015). Washington, DC: National Center for Education Statistics, Institute of Education Sciences, U.S. Department of Education.

Staklis, S., & Chen, X. (2010). *Profile of undergraduate students: Trends from selected years, 1995–96 to 2007–08* (NCES 2010-220). Washington, DC: National Center for Education Statistics, Institute of Education Sciences, U.S. Department of Education. Retrieved from http://nces.ed.gov/pubs2010/2010220.pdf

U.S. Department of Education. 2009 Integrated Postsecondary Education Data System (IPEDS). Washington, DC: National Center for Education Statistics. Retrieved from http://nces.ed.gov

Chapter 1. Anticipating College: Goals and Expectations

Camblin, S. J., Gullatt, Y., & Klopott, S. (2003). *Strategies for success: Six stories of increasing college access.* Retrieved from http://www.pathwaystocollege.net/pdf/StrategiesforSuccess_CaseStudies.pdf

Jobs for the Future. (2011). *Making the grade: Texas early college high schools prepare students for college.* Boston, MA: Author. Retrieved from http://www.jff.org/sites/default/files/MakingTheGrade-032311.pdf

Kirst, M. W., & Venezia, A. (Eds.). (2004). *From high school to college: Improving opportunities for success in postsecondary education.* San Francisco, CA: Wiley and Sons.

Lozano, A., Watt, K. M., & Huerta, J. (2009). A comparison study of 12th grade Hispanic students' college anticipations, aspirations, and college preparatory measures. *American Secondary Education, 38*(1). Retrieved from http://www.avid.org/dl/res_research/research_12thgradehispanic.pdf

Pascarella, E. T., & Terenzini, P. T. (2005). *How college affects students: A third decade of research* (Vol. 2). San Francisco, CA: Jossey-Bass.

Polinsky, T. L. (2003). Understanding student retention through a look at student goals, intentions, and behaviors. *Journal of College Student Retention, 4*(4), 261–276.

Terenzini, P., Rendón, L. I., Upcraft, L., Gregg, P., & Jalomo, R. (1996). Making the transition to college. In M. G. Weimer & R. Menges (Eds.), *Teaching on solid ground: Using scholarship to improve practice* (pp. 43–73). San Francisco, CA: Jossey-Bass.

Chapter 2. Ready or Not

Achieve, Inc. (2007). *Aligned expectations? A closer look at college admissions and placement tests.* Reprinted with permission. Retrieved from http://www.achieve.org/files/Admissions_and_Placement_FINAL2.pdf

Adelman, C. (2004). *Principal indicators of student academic histories in postsecondary education, 1972–2000.* Washington, DC: Institute of Education Sciences, U.S. Department of Education.

Adelman, C. (2006). *The toolbox revisited: Paths to degree completion from high school through college.* Washington, DC: U.S. Department of Education.

American Institutes for Research/SRI International. (2009). *Fifth annual early college high school initiative evaluation synthesis report. Six years and counting: The ECHSI matures.* Washington, DC: American Institutes for Research.

Bailey, T., Jeong, D. W., & Cho, S. (2008). *Referral, enrollment, and completion in developmental education sequences in community colleges* (CCRC Working Paper No. 15). New York, NY: Columbia University, Teachers College, Community College Research Center.

Bailey, T. R., & Karp, M. M. (2003). *Promoting college access and success: A review of credit-based transition programs.* Washington, DC: U.S. Department of Education.

Boroch, D., Hope, L., Smith, B., Gabriner, R., Mery, P., Johnstone, R., & Asera, R. (2010). *Student success in community colleges: A practical guide to developmental education.* San Francisco, CA: Jossey-Bass.

Boylan, H. R. (2002). *What works: Research-based best practices in developmental education.* Boone, NC: Continuous Quality Improvement Network with the National Center for Developmental Education, Appalachian State University.

Boylan, H. R. (2008). Relentless leader's focus on developmental education: An interview with Byron McClenney. *Journal of Developmental Education, 31*(3), 16–18.

Bressoud, D. (2012). *Why is the transition from high school to college important? Issues and next steps.* Paper presented at the Joint Math Meetings, Boston, MA. Retrieved from http://www.macalester.edu/~bressoud/talks/2012/MAA-NCTM.pdf

Collins, M. L. (2011). *College: Ready or not?* (21st Century Commission on the Future of Community Colleges Working Briefs). Washington, DC: American Association of Community Colleges.

Conley, D. (2010). *College and career ready: Helping all students succeed beyond high school.* San Francisco, CA: Jossey-Bass.

Edgecombe, N. (2011). *Accelerating the academic achievement of students referred to developmental education* (CCRC Working Paper No. 30). New York, NY: Columbia University, Teachers College, Community College Research Center.

Edwards, L., & Hughes, K. (2011). *Dual enrollment guide.* A joint publication of the Career Academy Support Network, University of California at Berkeley, and Institute on Education and the Economy, Teachers College, Columbia University. Berkeley, CA: Career Academy Support Network.

Ewing, M. (2006). *The AP® program and student outcomes: A summary of research* (RN-29, November 2006). Retrieved from http://professionals.collegeboard.com/profdownload/pdf/RN-29.pdf

Hoffman, N., Vargas, J., Venezia, A., & Miller, M. (2007). *Minding the gap: Why integrating high school with college makes sense and how to do it.* Cambridge, MA: Harvard University Press.

Jobs for the Future. (2010). *Spotlight on research. Early college graduates: Adapting, thriving and leading in college.* Boston, MA: Author. Retrieved from http://www.jff.org/sites/default/files/ECPrepareGradtoThriveCollege_032411.pdf

Karp, M. M., Calcagno, J. C., Hughes, K., Jeong, D. W., & Bailey, T. R. (2007). *The postsecondary achievement of participants in dual enrollment: An analysis of student outcomes in two states.* Louisville, KY: National Research Center for Career and Technical Education. Retrieved from http://136.165.122.102/UserFiles/File/pubs/Dual_Enrollment.pdf

Kirst, M. W. (2001). *Overcoming the high school senior slump: New education policies. Perspectives in public policy: Connecting higher education and the public schools.*

Washington, DC: Institute for Educational Leadership and National Center for Public Policy and Higher Education.

Kirst, M. W., & Bracco, K. R. (2004). Bridging the great divide: How the K–12 postsecondary split hurts students, and what can be done about it. In M. W. Kirst & A. Venezia (Eds.), *From high school to college: Improving opportunities for success in postsecondary education* (pp. 1–30). San Francisco, CA: Wiley and Sons.

Muraskin, L. (2010). *Effective college access programs: GEAR UP as a laboratory for change.* Retrieved from https://edsurveys.rti.org/gearup/ls/Muraskin_Final.pdf

Nodine, T. (2009). *Innovations in college readiness.* Boston, MA: Jobs for the Future.

Pascarella, E. T., & Terenzini, P. T. (2005). *How college affects students: A third decade of research* (Vol. 2). San Francisco, CA: Jossey-Bass.

Roueche, J. E., Ely, E. E., & Roueche, S. D. (2001). *In pursuit of excellence: The community college of Denver.* Washington, DC: Community College Press, American Association of Community Colleges.

Roueche, J. E., & Roueche, S. D. (1999). *High stakes, high performance: Making remedial education work.* Washington, DC: Community College Press, American Association of Community Colleges.

Rutschow, E. Z., & Schneider, E. (2011). *Unlocking the gate: What we know about improving developmental education.* New York, NY: MDRC.

Tierney, W. G., Bailey, T., Constantine, J., Finkelstein, N., & Hurd, N. F. (2009). *Helping students navigate the path to college: What high schools can do: A practice guide* (NCEE #2009-4066). Washington, DC: National Center for Education Evaluation and Regional Assistance, Institute of Education Sciences, U.S. Department of Education. Retrieved from http://ies.ed.gov/ncee/wwc/practiceguide.aspx?sid=11

Wathington, H., Barnett, E., Weissman, E., Teres, J., Pretlow, J., & Nakanishi, A. (2011). *Getting ready for college: An implementation and early impacts study of eight Texas developmental summer bridge programs.* New York, NY: National Center for Postsecondary Research, Columbia University, Teachers College, Community College Research Center.

Zeidenberg, J., Jenkins, D., & Calcagno, J. S. (2007). *Do student success courses actually help community college students succeed?* (CCRC Brief 36). New York, NY: Columbia University, Teachers College, Community College Research Center.

Chapter 3. Taking It Personally

Braxton, J. M., & McClendon, S. A. (2001). The fostering of social integration and retention through institutional practice. *Journal of College Student Retention Research, Theory & Practice*, 3(1), 57–71.

Center for Community College Student Engagement *(CCCSE)*. (2007). *Highlights, 6*(3). Austin, TX: University of Texas at Austin, Community College Leadership Program. Retrieved from http://www.ccsse.org/center/resources/docs/publications/Jan2007.pdf

Karp, M. M. (2011). *Toward a new understanding of non-academic student support: Four mechanisms encouraging positive student outcomes in the community college* (CCRC Working Paper No. 28). New York, NY: Columbia University, Teachers College, Community College Resource Center.

Kuh, G. D., Schuh, J. S., Whitt, E. J., & Associates. (1991). *Involving colleges: Successful approaches to fostering student learning and personal development outside the classroom*. San Francisco, CA: Jossey-Bass.

O'Brien, C., & Shedd, J. (2001). *Getting through college: Voices of low-income and minority students in New England*. Washington, DC: The Institute for Higher Education Policy.

Pascarella, E. T., & Terenzini, P. T. (2005). *How college affects students: A third decade of research* (Vol. 2). San Francisco, CA: Jossey-Bass.

Rendón, L. I. (2009). *Sentipensante (sensing/thinking) pedagogy. Educating for wholeness, social justice and liberation*. Sterling, VA: Stylus Press.

Tinto, V. (1993). *Leaving college: Rethinking the causes and cures of student attrition* (2nd ed.). Chicago, IL: University of Chicago Press.

Chapter 4. First Steps on the Pathway

Achieve, Inc. (2007). *Aligned expectations? A closer look at college admissions and placement tests*. Reprinted with permission. Retrieved from http://www.achieve.org/files/Admissions_and_Placement_FINAL2.pdf

ACT. (2010). *What works in student retention? Fourth national survey. Community colleges report**. Retrieved from http://www.act.org/research/policymakers/pdf/droptables/CommunityColleges.pdf

Center for Community College Student Engagement *(CCCSE)*. (2007). *Starting right: A first look at engaging entering students*. Austin, TX: University of Texas at Austin, Community College Leadership Program.

Center for Community College Student Engagement *(CCCSE)*. (2008). *Imagine success: Engaging entering students*. Austin, TX: University of Texas at Austin, Community College Leadership Program.

Center for Community College Student Engagement *(CCCSE)*. (2009). *Benchmarking & benchmarks: Effective practice with entering students*. Austin, TX: University of Texas at Austin, Community College Leadership Program.

Jenkins, D., & Cho, S. (2012). *Get with the program: Accelerating community college students' entry into and completion of programs of study* (CCRC Working Paper No. 32). New York, NY: Columbia University, Teachers College, Community College Research Center.

Jenkins, D., & Weiss, M. J. (2011). *Charting pathways to completion for low-income community college students* (CCRC Working Paper No. 34). New York, NY: Columbia University, Teachers College, Community College Research Center.

Karp, M. M., O'Gara, L., & Hughes, K. L. (2008). *Do support services at community colleges encourage success or reproduce disadvantage? An exploratory study of students in* two community colleges. New York, NY: Columbia University, Teachers College, Community College Research Center. Retrieved from http://ccrc.tc.columbia.edu/Publication.asp?UID=571

Lowe, A., & Toney, M. (2001). Academic advising: Views of the givers and takers. *College Student Retention Research, Theory & Practice, 2*(2), 93–108.

Vivian, C. (2005). Advising the at-risk college student. *The Educational Forum, 69*(4), 336–351.

Chapter 5. Learning How To Succeed in College

Calcagno, J. C., Crosta, P., Bailey, T., & Jenkins, D. (2007). Stepping stones to a degree: The impact of enrollment pathways and milestones on community college students. *Research in Higher Education, 48*(7), 755–801.

Cho, S., & Karp, M. M. (2012). *Student success courses and educational outcomes at Virginia community colleges.* New York, NY: Columbia University, Teachers College, Community College Research Center.

Clery, S. (2010). *Data notes, attendance and completion patterns, 5*(2). Retrieved from http://www.achievingthedream.org

Florida Department of Education. (2006). *Taking student life skills course increases academic success* (Data Trend # 31). Tallahassee: Florida Department of Education. Retrieved from http://www.fldoe.org/cc/OSAS/DataTrendsResearch/DT31.pdf

Goldrick-Rab, S. (2007). *Promoting academic momentum at community colleges: Challenges and opportunities.* New York, NY: Columbia University, Teachers College, Community College Research Center. Retrieved from http://ccrc.tc.columbia.edu/Publication.asp?UID=492

Moore, R. (2003). Attendance and performance: How important is it for students to attend class? *Journal of College Science and Teaching, 32*(6), 367–371.

O'Gara, L., Karp, M. M., & Hughes, K. L. (2009). Student success courses in the community college: An exploratory study of student perspectives. *Community College Review, 36*(3), 195–218.

Ward-Roof, J. A., & Hatch, C. (Eds.). (2003). *Designing successful transitions: A guide for orienting students to college* (2nd ed.). (Monograph No. 13). Joint publication with the National Orientation Directors Association. Columbia, SC: University of South Carolina, National Resource Center for the First-Year Experience and Students in Transition.

Zeidenberg, J., Jenkins, D., & Calcagno, J. S. (2007). *Do student success courses actually help community college students succeed?* (CCRC Brief 36). New York, NY: Columbia University, Teachers College, Community College Research Center.

Chapter 6. Engaging in Learning: What Matters?

Astin, A. W. (1984). Student involvement: A developmental theory for higher education. *Journal of College Student Personnel, 25*(4), 297–308.

Barefoot, B. O., & Gardner, J. N. (Eds.). (2005). *Achieving and sustaining institutional excellence for the first year of college.* San Francisco, CA: Jossey-Bass.

Barkley, E. F. (2010). *Student engagement techniques: A handbook for college faculty.* San Francisco, CA: Jossey-Bass.

Barkley, E. F., Cross, K. P., & Major, C. H. (2005). *Collaborative learning techniques: A handbook for college faculty.* San Francisco, CA: Jossey-Bass.

Chickering, A. W., & Gamson, Z. F. (1987). Seven principles for good practice in undergraduate education. *AAHE Bulletin, 39*(7), 3–7.

Dunlap, L., & Pettitt, M. (2008). Assessing student outcomes in learning communities: Two decades of studies at a community college. *Journal of Applied Research in the Community College, 15*(2), 140–149.

Guarasci, R. (2001). Recentering learning: An interdisciplinary approach to academic and student affairs. Understanding the role of academic and student collaboration in creating a successful learning environment. *New Directions for Higher Education, 116,* 101–109.

Jenkins, D., & Cho, S. (2012). *Get with the program: Accelerating community college students' entry into and completion of programs of study* (CCRC Working Paper No. 32). New York, NY: Columbia University, Teachers College, Community College Research Center.

Kuh, G. D., Kinzie, J., Schuh, J. H., & Whitt, E. J. (2005). *Student success in college: Creating conditions that matter.* San Francisco, CA: Jossey-Bass.

Navarro, D. J., Smith, M., George, B., & London, R.A. (2006). *Policy and institutional issues related to the Digital Bridge Academy replication.* Santa Cruz, CA: Center for Justice, Tolerance and Community. Retrieved from http://cbacademy.squarespace.com/storage/documents/effectiveness-studies/DBA%20Policy%20Report%20v5x-FINAL.pdf

Rendón, L. I. (2009). *Sentipensante (sensing/thinking) pedagogy. Educating for wholeness, social justice and liberation.* Sterling, VA: Stylus Press.

Roueche, J. E., Milliron, M. D., & Roueche, S. D. (2003). *Practical magic: On the front lines of teaching excellence.* Washington, DC: Community College Press, American Association of Community Colleges.

Scrivener, S., Bloom, D., LeBlanc, A., Paxson, C., Rouse, C. E., & Sommo, C. (2008). *A good start: Two-year effects of a freshman learning community program at Kingsborough Community College.* New York, NY: MDRC.

Smith, B. L. (2004). Beyond the revolving door: Learning communities and the first two years of college. In R. Kazis, J. Vargas, & N. Hoffman (Eds.), *Double the numbers: Increasing postsecondary credentials for underrepresented youth* (pp. 231–239). Cambridge, MA: Harvard Education Press.

Taylor, K., Moore, W., MacGregor, J., & Lindblad, J. (2003). *Learning communities research and assessment: What we know now.* National Learning Communities Project Monograph Series. Olympia, WA: The Evergreen State College, Washington Center for Improving the Quality of Undergraduate Education, in cooperation with the American Association for Higher Education.

Tinto, V. (1997). Classrooms as communities: Exploring the educational character of student persistence. *Journal of Higher Education, 68*(6), 599–623.

Tinto, V. (2012, in press). *Completing college: Rethinking institutional action.* Chicago, IL: University of Chicago Press.

Chapter 7. Disengaging: Now You See Me, Now You Don't

Bailey, T., Jaggars, S. S., & Jenkins, D. (2011). *Introduction to the CCRC assessment of evidence series.* New York, NY: Columbia University, Teachers College, Community College Resource Center.

Barefoot, B. O. (2004). Higher education's revolving door: Confronting the problem of student drop out in U.S. colleges and universities. *Open Learning, 19*(1), 9–18.

Berkner, L., & Choy, S. (2008). *Descriptive summary of 2003–04 beginning postsecondary students: Three years later* (NCES 2008-174). Washington, DC: National Center for Education Statistics, Institute of Education Sciences, U.S. Department of Education.

Goldrick-Rab, S. (2010). Challenges and opportunities for improving community college student success. *Review of Educational Research, 80*(3), 437–469.

Jenkins, D., & Weiss, M. J. (2011). *Charting pathways to completion for low-income community college students* (CCRC Working Paper No. 34). New York, NY: Columbia University, Teachers College, Community College Research Center.

Lundquist, C., Spalding, R. J., & Landrum, R. E. (2003). College student's thoughts about leaving the university: The impact of faculty attitudes and behaviors. *Journal of College Student Retention: Research, Theory & Practice, 4*(2), 123–133.

Offenstein, J., Moore, C., & Shulock, N. (2010). *Advancing by degrees: A framework for increasing college completion.* Sacramento, CA: Institute for Higher Education Leadership & Policy. Retrieved from http://www.collegeproductivity.org/sites/default/files/R_AdvbyDegrees_0510.pdf

Radford, A. W., Berkner, L., Wheeless, S. C., & Shepherd, B. (2010). *Persistence and attainment of 2003–04 beginning postsecondary students: After 6 years* (NCES 2011-151). Washington, DC: National Center for Education Statistics. Retrieved from http://nces.ed.gov/pubs2011/2011151.pdf

Scott-Clayton, J. (2011). *The shapeless river: Does a lack of structure inhibit students' progress at community colleges?* (CCRC Working Paper No. 25). New York, NY: Columbia University, Teachers College, Community College Resource Center.

Tinto, V. (1993). *Leaving college: Rethinking the causes and cures of student attrition* (2nd ed.). Chicago, IL: University of Chicago Press.

Chapter 8. Community Colleges: Doing What Works for Students

Bailey, T., Jaggars, S. S., & Jenkins, D. (2011). *Introduction to the CCRC assessment of evidence series.* New York, NY: Columbia University, Teachers College, Community College Resource Center.

Bloom, D., & Sommo, C. (2005). *Building learning communities: Early results from the opening doors demonstration at Kingsborough Community College*. New York, NY: MDRC.

Center for Community College Student Engagement *(CCCSE)*. (2012). *A matter of degrees: Promising practices for community college student success (A first look)*. Austin, TX: University of Texas at Austin, Community College Leadership Program.

Center for Community College Student Engagement *(CCCSE)*. (2012). *Resources and publications*. Austin, TX: University of Texas at Austin, Community College Leadership Program. Retrieved from http://www.ccsse.org/center/resources/publications.cfm

Jenkins, D., Jaggars, S. S., & Roksa, J. (2009). *Promoting gatekeeper course success among community college students needing remediation: Findings and recommendations from a Virginia study*. New York, NY: Columbia University, Teachers College, Community College Research Center.

Karp, M. M., O'Gara, L., & Hughes, K. L. (2008). *Do support services at community colleges encourage success or reproduce disadvantage? An exploratory study of students in two community colleges*. New York, NY: Columbia University, Teachers College, Community College Research Center. Retrieved from http://ccrc.tc.columbia.edu/Publication.asp?UID=571

Kerrigan, M. R., & Slater, D. (2010). *Collaborating to create change: How El Paso community college improved the readiness of its incoming students through Achieving the Dream* (Report no. 4 in Culture of Evidence Series). New York, NY: Columbia University, Teachers College, Community College Research Center.

Scrivener, S., Bloom, D., LeBlanc, A., Paxson, C., Rouse, C. E., & Sommo, C. (2008). *A good start: Two-year effects of a freshman learning community program at Kingsborough Community College*. New York, NY: MDRC.

Chapter 9. Listening, Learning, Acting

Bailey, T., Jaggars, S. S., & Jenkins, D. (2011). *Introduction to the CCRC assessment of evidence series*. New York, NY: Columbia University, Teachers College, Community College Resource Center.

Barefoot, B. O., & Gardner, J. N. (Eds.). (2005). *Achieving and sustaining institutional excellence for the first year of college*. San Francisco, CA: Jossey-Bass.

Brownell, J. E., & Swaner, L. E. (2010*). Five high-impact practices: Research on learning outcomes, completion, and quality*. Washington, DC: Association of American Colleges and Universities.

Center for Community College Student Engagement *(CCCSE)*. (2012). *A matter of degrees: Promising practices for community college student success (A first look)*. Austin, TX: University of Texas at Austin, Community College Leadership Program.

Center for Community College Student Engagement *(CCCSE)*. (2012). *Focus group toolkit*. Austin, TX: University of Texas at Austin, Community College Leadership Program. Retrieved from http://www.ccsse.org/center/iss/focusgrouptoolkit.cfm

Fullan, M. (2001). *Leading in a culture of change.* San Francisco, CA: Jossey-Bass.

Jenkins, D. (2011). *Redesigning community colleges for completion: Lessons from research on high-performance organizations* (CCRC Working Paper No. 24). New York, NY: Columbia University, Teachers College, Community College Resource Center.

Jenkins, D., & Cho, S. (2012). *Get with the program: Accelerating community college students' entry into and completion of programs of study* (CCRC Working Paper No. 32). New York, NY: Columbia University, Teachers College, Community College Research Center.

Kuh, G. D., Kinzie, J., Schuh, J. H., & Whitt, E. J. (2005). *Student success in college: Creating conditions that matter.* San Francisco, CA: Jossey-Bass.

McClenney, K. (2004). Redefining quality in community colleges: Focusing on good educational practice. *Change 36*(6), 16–21.

McClenney, K., & Oriano, A. (2012). From promising to high-impact: Evaluating educational practices in the community college for increased student success. *Community College Journal,* April/May. Washington, DC: American Association of Community Colleges.

O'Banion, T. (1997). *A learning college for the 21st century.* Phoenix, AZ: American Council on Education and The Oryx Press.

Offenstein, J., Moore, C., & Shulock, N. (2010). *Advancing by degrees: A framework for increasing college completion.* Sacramento, CA: Institute for Higher Education Leadership & Policy. Retrieved from http://www.collegeproductivity.org/sites/default/files/R_AdvbyDegrees_0510.pdf

Scott-Clayton, J. (2011). *The shapeless river: Does a lack of structure inhibit students' progress at community colleges?* (CCRC Working Paper No. 25). New York, NY: Columbia University, Teachers College, Community College Resource Center.

Tinto, V. (2012, in press). *Completing college: Rethinking institutional action.* Chicago, IL: University of Chicago Press.

Resources

The observations made in this book are richly informed by the work of an array of multiyear national, regional, and state initiatives focused on college readiness and community college student success. The list below contains brief descriptions of organizations and projects where college leaders can find additional information.

ACE — Academy for College Excellence (formerly Digital Bridge Academy)

http://www.cabrillo.edu/academics/ace

The Academy for College Excellence (ACE) develops strategies to help community colleges identify the ways that they currently work with underprepared students, assess their existing approaches, and support changes to increase effectiveness with these students. ACE is a full-time, first-semester community college program that targets the needs of underprepared students while equipping them to succeed in the technology-driven, 21st-century economy. A highly collaborative enterprise that teaches teamwork and personal responsibility, the ACE approach also promotes individual self-exploration, self-improvement, and persistence.

Achieve, Inc.

http://www.achieve.org

Achieve is an independent, bi-partisan, nonprofit education reform organization led by governors and business leaders.

American Diploma Project

In 2005, Achieve launched the American Diploma Project Network, through which governors, state education officials, postsecondary leaders, and business executives work together to improve postsecondary preparation. The Network is committed to a common core set of standards and encourages four critical actions: aligning high school standards and assessments with the knowledge and skills required for success after high school, requiring all high school graduates to complete a college- and career-ready curriculum so that earning a diploma ensures that a student is prepared for opportunities after high school, building assessments into the statewide system that measure students' readiness for college and careers, and developing an accountability system that promotes college and career readiness.

Achieving the Dream

http://www.achievingthedream.org

Achieving the Dream, Inc., is a national nonprofit organization dedicated to helping more community college students, particularly low-income students and students of color, stay in school and earn a college certificate or degree. Evidence-based, student-centered, and built on the values of equity and excellence, Achieving the Dream is closing achievement gaps and accelerating student success nationwide.

Association of American Colleges and Universities

http://www.aacu.org

AAC&U is a national association concerned with the quality, vitality, and public standing of undergraduate liberal education. Its members are committed to extending the advantages of a liberal education to all students, regardless of academic specialization or intended career. AAC&U comprises more than 1,250 member institutions — including accredited public and private colleges, community colleges, and universities.

Pathways to College Network

http://www.pathwaystocollege.net

AAC&U is a lead partner in the Pathways to College Network, an alliance of national organizations that advances college opportunity for underserved students by raising public awareness, supporting innovative research, and promoting evidence-based policies and practices across the K–12 and higher education sectors. Pathways promotes the use of research-based policies and practices; the development of new research that is both rigorous and actionable; and the alignment of efforts across middle school, high school, and higher education in order to promote college access and success for underserved students.

Developing a Community College Student Roadmap: From Entrance to Engagement in Educational Achievement and Success

http://www.aacu.org/roadmap/index.cfm

Developing a Community College Student Roadmap is a project of AAC&U's Liberal Education and America's Promise (LEAP), a public advocacy, campus action, and research initiative. The Roadmap Project works intensively with 12 community colleges that are striving to create an integrated roadmap to support both student persistence and higher levels of academic achievement. These colleges are developing and coordinating practices and policies to support engaged learning, provide meaningful assessment data about student learning outcomes, and help build a community of support for high achievement.

AVID — Advancement Via Individual Determination

http://www.avid.org

AVID is an elementary-through-postsecondary college readiness system designed to increase school-wide learning and performance. The AVID system accelerates student learning, uses research-based methods of effective instruction, provides meaningful and motivational professional development, and serves as a catalyst for systemic reform and change.

California Community Colleges Basic Skills Initiative (BSI)

http://www.cccbsi.org

The Basic Skills Initiative (BSI) was designed to improve student access and success in California's community colleges. The project addresses credit and noncredit basic skills and supports professional development for faculty and staff in basic skills and English as a Second Language (ESL). BSI provides online resources and examples of effective practices for educators and policymakers.

Carnegie Foundation for the Advancement of Teaching

http://www.carnegiefoundation.org

The Carnegie Foundation for the Advancement of Teaching is an independent policy and research center focused on improving teaching and learning. Carnegie's current improvement research approach builds on the scholarship of teaching and learning by building organizational capacity and encouraging the sharing of practices that show promise in improving student success.

Quantway/Statway Math Pathways

Carnegie's Quantway/Statway initiative is developing two new approaches to mathematics: one-year courses that build quantitative literacy (Quantway) and statistical proficiency (Statway). Within both of these pathways, the initiative is infusing teaching strategies that build students' confidence as math learners.

The Center for Community College Student Engagement

http://www.cccse.org

The Center for Community College Student Engagement *(CCCSE)*, a research and service initiative of the Community College Leadership Program in the College of Education at The University of Texas at Austin, provides information about effective educational practice in community colleges. The Center assists institutions and policymakers in using data and information about effective practices to promote improvements in student learning, persistence, and attainment. The Center administers student surveys: the Community College Survey of Student Engagement *(CCSSE)* and the Survey of Entering Student Engagement *(SENSE)*. The Center also administers the Community College Faculty Survey of Student Engagement *(CCFSSE)*.

CCSSE benchmarks focus on institutional practices and student behaviors that promote student engagement and that are positively related to student learning and persistence. The five benchmarks are: active and collaborative learning, student effort, academic challenge, student-faculty interaction, and support for learners. *SENSE* benchmarks focus on institutional practices and student behaviors that promote student engagement early in the college experience. The six benchmarks are: early connections, high expectations and aspirations, clear academic plan and pathway, effective track to college readiness, engaged learning, and academic and social support network.

Initiative on Student Success

http://www.ccsse.org/center/iss/index.cfm

The *Initiative on Student Success*, the qualitative arm of the Center, brings to life the community college experience by conducting focus groups and interviews with community college students, faculty, staff, and presidents.

Identifying and Promoting High-Impact Educational Practices

http://www.ccsse.org/center/highimpact

The Center has undertaken a large-scale research and practice-improvement initiative focused on Identifying and Promoting High-Impact Educational Practices in Community Colleges. As part of this initiative, the Center now administers the Community College Institutional Survey (CCIS). Using results from its surveys, the Center also studies whether participation in high-impact educational practices varies across subgroups of students and how student participation in these practices is related to overall student engagement, academic progress, and college completion.

CFES — College for Every Student

http://www.collegefes.org

Since its founding in 1991, CFES has helped thousands of underserved students in 540 K–12 public schools nationwide take steps toward college. Through its mentoring, school-college partnerships, and student leadership programs, CFES seeks to raise students' academic performance and educational aspirations so that more students will graduate from high school and go on to succeed in college.

College Summit

http://www.collegesummit.org

College Summit works in partnership with schools, school districts, and colleges to develop a sustainable model for raising college enrollment rates community-wide. The organization helps educators embed a postsecondary planning structure and resources into each school. This includes a regular, for-credit College Summit class with detailed curriculum, regular teacher training, and online tools to help both teachers and students manage college applications online. Data and accountability tools help educators innovate and make course corrections midstream to maximize the potential for more students to go on to college.

Community College Research Center

http://ccrc.tc.columbia.edu

CCRC's mission is to conduct research on the major issues affecting community colleges in the United States and to contribute to the development of practice and policy that expands access to higher education and promotes success for all students. CCRC's extensive body of research provides a strong foundation on which to build new policies and initiatives to improve outcomes for community college students.

Completion Matters

http://www.completionmatters.org

Completion Matters is a project created in 2010 by the Institute for the Study of Knowledge Management in Education (ISKME). Dedicated to the study, spread, and strategic use of knowledge management in education, ISKME helps schools, colleges, universities, and the organizations that support them expand their capacity to collect and share information, apply it to well-defined problems, and create open knowledge-driven environments focused on learning and success.

The Education Trust

http://www.edtrust.org

The Education Trust promotes high academic achievement for all students at all levels — prekindergarten through college. The organization's goal is to close the gaps in opportunity and achievement for students from low-income families and students who are black, Latino, or American Indian. Additionally, The Education Trust works with policy leaders to fulfill the purpose of Pell Grants and Head Start while examining the role of financial assistance in student persistence.

Foundations of Excellence in the First College Year

http://www.fyfoundations.org

Foundations of Excellence is a comprehensive, externally guided self-study and improvement process for the first year of college. Guided by a campus-based task force, the work begins with a campus audit of the first year for new and transfer students — the "Current Practices Inventory," continues with a 9- to 12-month process of evaluation using the Foundational Dimensions and related performance indicators, and culminates in the development of a strategic action plan for campus improvement.

Gulf Coast PASS

http://utcclp.org

Under the leadership of *Student Success Initiatives,* part of the Community College Leadership Program (CCLP) at The University of Texas at Austin, eight Gulf Coast (Houston-area) community colleges involved in Achieving the Dream have been awarded grants to support a three-year initiative focused on their work with 11 partner school districts to increase college readiness among high school graduates, ease the transition for graduates to community colleges, and increase student success in developmental education courses. With support from Houston Endowment Inc., partners in the initiative include the CCLP, Houston A+ Challenge, Institute for Evidence-Based Change, eight community college districts, and 11 independent school districts in the Houston/Gulf Coast area. For more information, call 512-471-7545.

Houston A+ Challenge

http://www.houstonaplus.org

Houston A+ Challenge serves as a catalyst for change in the public schools throughout the Houston, TX region. The organization teams with principals and teachers in targeted schools to provide the tools they need to help every student prepare for postsecondary success.

IEBC – Institute for Evidence-Based Change

http://www.iebcnow.org

The Institute for Evidence-Based Change helps education stakeholders — K–12 school systems, community colleges, universities, employers, child welfare systems, and others — use data to boost student achievement. IEBC helps individuals and organizations become more skilled at making informed decisions, improving practice, and increasing student success.

Jobs for the Future

http://www.jff.org

Jobs for the Future (JFF) identifies, develops, and promotes education and workforce strategies that expand opportunity for youth and adults who are struggling to advance. In more than 200 communities across 43 states, JFF works to improve the pathways leading from high school to college to family-sustaining careers.

Early College High School Initiative

Early College is a bold approach to high school reform, based on the principle that academic rigor, combined with the opportunity to save time and money, is a powerful motivator for students to work hard and meet serious intellectual challenges. Early College schools blend high school and college in a rigorous yet supportive program, compressing the time it takes to complete a high school diploma and the first two years of college. Today, the Early College High School Initiative includes 270 schools serving more than 75,000 students in 28 states.

The League for Innovation in the Community College

http://www.league.org

The League is an international organization that hosts conferences and institutes, develops web resources, conducts research, produces publications, provides services, and leads projects and initiatives with its member colleges, corporate partners, and other agencies.

Significant Discussions

The Significant Discussions Project is based on the recognition that misalignment of curriculum among secondary schools, community colleges, universities, and employers creates barriers to student success and that collaborative discussions about curriculum alignment across educational sectors are often random and voluntary. The first phase of the project resulted in the development of *Significant Discussions: A Guide for Secondary and Postsecondary Curriculum Alignment,* designed to facilitate discussions between faculty and administrators in secondary and postsecondary institutions that would lead to curriculum alignment between these institutions. Within the current phase of work, nine community colleges and their feeder schools are partnering to develop aligned mathematics curricula.

MDRC

http://www.mdrc.org

MDRC evaluates the effectiveness of policies and programs designed to help students succeed. The organization's current community college research agenda includes a focus on the following interventions: improvement of developmental education, learning communities, institutional reform, revisions to financial aid policies and information, and improvements in guidance counseling and other support services.

National College Access Network (NCAN)

http://www.collegeaccess.org

NCAN's mission is to build, strengthen, and empower communities committed to college access and success so that all students, especially those underrepresented in postsecondary education, can achieve their educational dreams. NCAN helps its members serve students better by providing programs with up-to-date tools and resources, connecting them to each other, and informing them of developments in the field.

Phi Theta Kappa Honor Society

http://www.ptk.org

Phi Theta Kappa recognizes and encourages scholarship among two-year college students. The Society provides opportunities for individual growth and development through participation in honors, leadership, service, and fellowship programming.

The Washington Center for Improving the Quality of Undergraduate Education: Learning Communities National Resource Center at Evergreen State College

http://www.evergreen.edu/washcenter

This national directory of learning communities provides information about institutions across the United States that offer learning community programs. In addition to the directory, the Washington Center also provides a residential summer institute for campus teams, a bank of resources on implementation and assessment, and publications on implementation and assessment.

ABOUT THE AUTHORS

KAY M. McCLENNEY

Kay M. McClenney is director of the Center for Community College Student Engagement, part of the Community College Leadership Program (CCLP) at The University of Texas at Austin. The Center conducts the Community College Survey of Student Engagement *(CCSSE)* and the Survey of Entering Student Engagement *(SENSE)* and has surveyed nearly 2 million community college students at more than 800 colleges in 50 states. The survey research is complemented by findings from student focus groups conducted across the country since 2002.

Also within the CCLP, McClenney is senior consultant to the University of Texas/CCLP work on the national Achieving the Dream initiative and co-director of Student Success BY THE NUMBERS. She was co-director of CLASS — the California Leadership Alliance for Student Success — and of the national Bridges to Opportunity initiative. She previously served for 10 years as vice president of the Education Commission of the States and for a number of years as a community college educator, including roles as faculty member, program director, system administrator, and interim CEO.

She earned her Ph.D. in educational administration from the CCLP at The University of Texas at Austin. She holds a B.A. from Trinity University and an M.A. in Psychology from Texas Christian University.

She has served as a member of the board of directors of the American Association of Community Colleges (AACC) and the executive board of the American Association for Women in Community Colleges (AAWCC). She received the 2002 PBS O'Banion Prize for contributions to teaching and learning in America, the 2009 Mildred Bulpitt Woman of the Year Award from the AAWCC, the 2009 International Leadership Award from the National Institute for Staff and Organizational Development (NISOD), and the 2011 National Leadership Award from AACC. She co-chaired AACC's 21st Century Commission on the Future of Community Colleges.

ARLEEN ARNSPARGER

Arleen Arnsparger is project manager of the *Initiative on Student Success* at the Center for Community College Student Engagement at The University of Texas at Austin. In her role leading the qualitative work of the Center, Arnsparger works with community colleges throughout the country, conducting focus groups and interviews with students to learn about their college experiences, interviewing presidents, and listening to faculty and staff.

Since her early career as a TV and radio reporter and newscaster, she has been a professional listener! Arnsparger asks questions that get to the heart of people's perceptions, experiences, and actions.

A frequent keynote speaker and facilitator, Arnsparger has served as a consultant to educational institutions and other organizations whose leaders are striving to improve performance and build capacity within their organizations.

Arnsparger previously served as an administrator at community colleges in New York and Colorado and as an adjunct faculty member in both two- and four-year institutions. As an education policy advisor, she worked with governors, state leaders, higher education systems, and school districts throughout the country on education improvement. In that role, Arnsparger co-authored *How to Deal with Community Criticism of School Change, Building Community Support for Schools: A Practical Guide to Strategic Communications,* and *Do-It-Yourself Focus Groups: A Low-Cost Way to Listen to Your Community.*

In addition to her work in the community college sector, Arnsparger writes and speaks about how to bridge generational differences in the workplace. She is the co-author of the books *Millennials@Work: Engaging the New Generation* and *4genR8tns: Succeeding with Colleagues, Cohorts & Customers.*

The content of this DVD will help bring student voices into campus conversations. The DVD contains a 12-minute video highlighting students' early experiences in the community college, along with individual video segments that address specific topics and may be used to prompt discussions or augment college presentations. Also included is a focus group toolkit intended to help college administrators, faculty, and staff listen to their students.

Students Speak — Let's Listen Well!